Readings on Eugen

WITHDRAWN

ON LINE

JEFFERSON TWP. PUBLIC LIBRARY
1031 Weldon Road
Oak Ridge, NJ 07438-9511

(973) 208-6115

DEMCO

READINGS ON

EUGENE O'NEILL

THE GREENHAVEN PRESS
Literary Companion
TO AMERICAN AUTHORS

EUGENE O'NEILL

David Bender, *Publisher*
Bruno Leone, *Executive Editor*
Brenda Stalcup, *Managing Editor*
Bonnie Szumski, *Series Editor*
Thomas Siebold, *Book Editor*

Greenhaven Press, San Diego, CA

Library of Congress Cataloging-in-Publication Data

Readings on Eugene O'Neill / Thomas Siebold, book editor.
      p.   cm. — (The Greenhaven Press literary
   companion to American authors)
      Includes bibliographical references and index.
      ISBN 1-56510-655-5 (alk. paper). —
   ISBN 1-56510-654-7 (pbk. : alk. paper)
      1. O'Neill, Eugene, 1888–1953—Criticism and inter-
   pretation. I. Siebold, Thomas. II. Series.
   PS3529.N5Z7977   1998
   812'.52—dc21   97-28011
                                                        CIP

Every effort has been made to trace the owners of copyrighted material. The articles in this volume may have been edited for content, length, and/or reading level. The titles have been changed to enhance the editorial purpose of the Opposing Viewpoints® concept. Those interested in locating the original source will find the complete citation on the first page of each article.

Cover photo: Archive Photos

Copyright ©1998 by Greenhaven Press, Inc.
PO Box 289009
San Diego, CA 92198-9009
Printed in the U.S.A.

"The tragedy of life is what makes it worthwhile."

Eugene O'Neill

Contents

FOREWORD

> *"'Tis the good reader that*
> *makes the good book."*
>
> Ralph Waldo Emerson

The story's bare facts are simple: The captain, an old and scarred seafarer, walks with a peg leg made of whale ivory. He relentlessly drives his crew to hunt the world's oceans for the great white whale that crippled him. After a long search, the ship encounters the whale and a fierce battle ensues. Finally the captain drives his harpoon into the whale, but the harpoon line catches the captain about the neck and drags him to his death.

A simple story, a straightforward plot—yet, since the 1851 publication of Herman Melville's *Moby-Dick*, readers and critics have found many meanings in the struggle between Captain Ahab and the whale. To some, the novel is a cautionary tale that depicts how Ahab's obsession with revenge leads to his insanity and death. Others believe that the whale represents the unknowable secrets of the universe and that Ahab is a tragic hero who dares to challenge fate by attempting to discover this knowledge. Perhaps Melville intended Ahab as a criticism of Americans' tendency to become involved in well-intentioned but irrational causes. Or did Melville model Ahab after himself, letting his fictional character express his anger at what he perceived as a cruel and distant god?

Although literary critics disagree over the meaning of *Moby-Dick*, readers do not need to choose one particular interpretation in order to gain an understanding of Melville's novel. Instead, by examining various analyses, they can gain numerous insights into the issues that lie under the surface of the basic plot. Studying the writings of literary critics can also aid readers in making their own assessments of *Moby-Dick* and other literary works and in developing analytical thinking skills.

The Greenhaven Literary Companion Series was created with these goals in mind. Designed for young adults, this unique anthology series provides an engaging and comprehensive introduction to literary analysis and criticism. The essays included in the Literary Companion Series are chosen for their accessibility to a young adult audience and are expertly edited in consideration of both the reading and comprehension levels of this audience. In addition, each essay is introduced by a concise summation that presents the contributing writer's main themes and insights. Every anthology in the Literary Companion Series contains a varied selection of critical essays that cover a wide time span and express diverse views. Wherever possible, primary sources are represented through excerpts from authors' notebooks, letters, and journals and through contemporary criticism.

Each title in the Literary Companion Series pays careful consideration to the historical context of the particular author or literary work. In-depth biographies and detailed chronologies reveal important aspects of authors' lives and emphasize the historical events and social milieu that influenced their writings. To facilitate further research, every anthology includes primary and secondary source bibliographies of articles and/or books selected for their suitability for young adults. These engaging features make the Greenhaven Literary Companion series ideal for introducing students to literary analysis in the classroom or as a library resource for young adults researching the world's great authors and literature.

Exceptional in its focus on young adults, the Greenhaven Literary Companion Series strives to present literary criticism in a compelling and accessible format. Every title in the series is intended to spark readers' interest in leading American and world authors, to help them broaden their understanding of literature, and to encourage them to formulate their own analyses of the literary works that they read. It is the editors' hope that young adult readers will find these anthologies to be true companions in their study of literature.

INTRODUCTION

Readings on Eugene O'Neill is designed to help students gain a greater appreciation of one of America's most significant playwrights. The carefully edited articles provide an overview of O'Neill's key ideas, his artistic philosophy, his impact on American theater, and his background as an individual and artist. Each of the literary essays is readable, manageable in length, and focuses on concepts suitable for a beginning exploration into the genre of literary criticism. Additionally, this diverse overview of O'Neill presents students with a wealth of material for writing reports, designing oral presentations, and enriching their understanding of drama as art.

An introduction to Eugene O'Neill is an important component in a student's study of American literature. More than any other modern playwright, O'Neill shaped and defined the nature and style of American theater. He broke from the melodrama and superficial realism that dominated the American stage through World War I by structuring his plays expressionistically, focusing on subjective emotions and ideas rather than on objective reality. With O'Neill, audiences saw American plays for the first time infused with modern psychology, controversial topics, and serious philosophical ideas. Playwrights who followed O'Neill looked to him as the starting point of serious twentieth-century theater in the United States.

The critical essays in *Readings on Eugene O'Neill* will help students to comprehend the meaning of O'Neill's plays and discover new methods of evaluating drama and appreciating the structure of dramatic form. By reading the interpretations of literary critics, students will develop a meaningful vocabulary for approaching fundamental literary questions about the playwright's themes, characters, philosophy, and language. They will also provide an important framework for understanding O'Neill's stature as a writer, the historical setting in which he wrote, and his place in the evolution of American theater history.

In addition to the essays, *Readings on Eugene O'Neill* provides other pertinent material about O'Neill's life and writing. The biographical sketch offers readers background into the author's life and how it influenced his work. The chronology outlines a useful overview of O'Neill's works and places them in an historical time frame. The bibliography identifies valuable resources for students who want to complete further research.

O'Neill's work generates a strong reaction from both his critics and his audiences. Because his plays were a radical departure from the typical plays of the day, and because he was continually experimenting with dramatic form, critics have had a hard time categorizing and appreciating O'Neill. With all of his plays, however, O'Neill's audiences are challenged to think about themselves and the circumstances that confront them. *Readings on Eugene O'Neill* organizes a critical look at O'Neill that is intended to be enjoyable, provocative, and instructive.

EUGENE O'NEILL: A BIOGRAPHY

After meeting Eugene O'Neill for the first time in 1926, critic Barrett H. Clark recorded his impression of the playwright:

> He is tall and slender and wiry, with long arms and strong hands. His body is lithe and might be thought awkward if it were not under perfect control. He is shy and diffident; he usually seems embarrassed; unless he is discussing what interests him, he speaks haltingly or not at all. His silences are long and eloquent. His face in repose has a chiselled but by no means cold severity; his smile is disarmingly frank and engaging. There is something at times almost impish in his low-toned comments, which are apt to be tinged with gleeful malice that's more a manner of talking than an expression of opinion. With the ordinary amenities of social intercourse he has no patience, yet no one would dream of calling him discourteous. What interests him and awakens his sympathy and imagination engrosses all his attentive faculties.

Clark, like most others who knew O'Neill, was initially mesmerized by the playwright's charm—his urbanity, his insightful humor, his intensity, his ability to tell picturesque stories, and his intellectual sensitivity. In 1926 O'Neill was on his way to becoming one of America's foremost dramatists. By the end of his career, he would write more than sixty plays and be awarded the Nobel Prize for literature; four of his plays would receive Pulitzer Prizes. More than any other playwright, O'Neill's style, subject matter, and theatrical vision would change the direction of American theater. Clark sensed at their first meeting that he was in the presence of a great dramatist, perhaps a talent of gigantic proportions.

O'Neill's success was born out of complexity. He was a tortured artist haunted by a family that was unorthodox and dysfunctional, often emotionally brutal; children whom he neglected and who suffered because of his neglect; three volatile marriages; crises precipitated by his brother's destructive alcoholism; and a nagging sense of personal failure.

He was also driven by a desire to know, to confront unanswerable questions about life, the human condition, and the eternal. His intellectual anguish and restlessness drove him to seek new experiences: He went to sea, lived in poverty on the waterfront, drank heavily, womanized, and wandered from one part of the country to another. He confronted life directly and, at times, self-destructively. He once wrote "I don't love life because it is pretty. Prettiness is only clothesdeep. I am a truer lover than that. I love it naked."

O'Neill's raw confrontation with life gave him the material for his plays. His adventures became the stuff of plots, people he knew and observed evolved into characters, and his tensions were played out in the themes of his plays. As an intensely autobiographical writer, O'Neill often used his plays to cope with his personal and psychological demons.

O'NEILL'S FAMILY

Eugene's father, James O'Neill, the son of an Irish immigrant who abandoned his family to return to Ireland, was an actor who possessed good looks, a robust voice, and a gregarious personality that often made him the center of attention. Although he showed promise as a classical actor, James found fame and wealth playing the lead in the melodramatic play *The Count of Monte Cristo*. Over the span of twenty-five years touring the country, James played the flamboyant, swashbuckling count in over six thousand performances. His life as an actor kept his family on the move throughout the fall and winter months, traveling by train and lodging in one hotel room after another. At the end of his life, as he lay dying in a Boston hotel, Eugene ironically referred to his early life touring with his father when he said, "Born in a hotel and died in a hotel." While on tour, James had little time or energy to be an attentive father, and family cohesiveness suffered as a result. The youngster Eugene, who resented their itinerant lifestyle, mockingly referred to his father as "Monte Cristo." In his autobiographical play *Long Day's Journey into Night*, Eugene summed up his father's plight as a "one-role actor" in a speech by James Tyrone, the father in the play who is reminiscent of James O'Neill; the play Tyrone bought for a song and rode to success in "ruined me with its promise of an easy fortune . . . and by the time I woke up to the fact I'd become a slave to the damned thing and did try other plays, it was too late, I'd lost the great talent I once had through years of easy repetition."

Eugene's mother, Ella Quinlan O'Neill, also disliked life on the road. Ella grew up in a comfortable middle-class family in Ohio, supported by her father, a successful businessman. Ella was a devout Catholic and had been educated in a convent. She was talented, beautiful, and, at one point, had the potential to become a concert pianist. But with a grudging sense of duty to her husband, Ella acquiesced to the not altogether respectable life of a traveling actor's wife. Ella never adjusted to this unconventional lifestyle however, and was often in poor health. She and James had three children: James (Jamie) Jr., born in 1878; Edmund, born in 1885; and Eugene, born on October 16, 1888. Edmund contracted measles from Jamie and died at one and a half. After Eugene was born, Ella's doctor gave her morphine to relieve postpartum depression. The drug momentarily assuaged her discomfort, but ultimately drove her to a hopeless, lifelong addiction. While preparing to write *Long Day's Journey into Night*, Eugene sketched out on a private sheet of notebook paper a summary of his mother's life: "Lonely life—spoiled before marriage . . . fashionable convent girl—religious & naive—talent for music—physical beauty—ostracism after marriage due to husband's profession—lonely life after marriage."

O'NEILL'S EARLY YEARS

When Eugene O'Neill was just a few months old, his parents brought him on a cross-country tour of *The Count of Monte Cristo*. Because his mother was often nervous, depressed, or incapacitated by drugs, Eugene was put under the care of a nurse named Sarah Sandy, who, although she was a good caretaker, was hardly a suitable substitute for friends or a mother. Reminiscing about his childhood, O'Neill remembered that Sandy would tell him scary stories about bloody murders, which in turn generated terrifying nightmares in the impressionable young Eugene. O'Neill's life of hotels, trains, and theaters kept him out of touch with other children; even Jamie had been sent away to boarding school. To help fend off loneliness, Eugene became an avid reader. Each spring, when the theater tour ended, the O'Neills retreated to their home in New London, Connecticut. Summer days at their pink clapboard cottage near Long Island Sound were comforting to young Eugene. Although his mother remained detached, James, relaxed away from the stage, showed genuine warmth and concern for his boys. Eugene and Jamie boated, swam, and read together along the coastline rocks. But the summers quickly ended and the loneliness of the tour resumed in the fall. At age seven, Eugene's parents sent him to St. Aloysius, a Catholic boarding school. The six years Eugene spent at St. Aloysius and another two-year stay at the New York Catholic De LaSalle Institute were years of intense feelings of rejection. O'Neill once stated that his boarding school days were defined by "outbursts of loneliness." Eugene remained a loner who rarely participated in the games of the other boys, instead spending most of his time reading or writing long letters to Jamie. In a moment of blunt recollection, O'Neill stated that "the truth is, that I had no childhood." Jamie, meanwhile, became increasingly cynical, depressed, and wild. To make matters worse, Eugene's mother fell further into her drug addiction and repeatedly entered sanatoriums for cures that did not work. At home during the summer of 1903, a panicked Ella, suffering from drug withdrawal, ran from their cottage with the intent of drowning herself in a nearby river. James and the two boys ran after her and dragged her home. The humiliating incident, which is related in *Long Day's Journey into Night*, forced Eugene to acknowledge that his mother was a drug addict.

At age fourteen, Eugene was sent to Betts Academy in Stamford, Connecticut, where he fared much better than at the Catholic schools. Betts was much more liberal and tolerant, accommodating Eugene's introverted personality. Here he read the classics voraciously. His favorite authors were Leo Tolstoy, Jack London, Joseph Conrad, and Oscar Wilde. Eugene meticulously kept a notebook in which he jotted down bits of dialogue, character sketches, and ideas that came into his head. As a close observer of the people and world around him, Eugene was developing the habits that would serve him well later as a dramatist. After he graduated from Betts, Eugene entered Princeton in 1906, but he lasted only nine months before he dropped out. Saying he felt restricted by the cloistered world of the tradition-laden school, he wrote of his short stay there, "We were not in touch with life or on the trail of real things, and that was one consideration that drove me out." Instead of studying, Eugene spent much of his time in taverns or cavorting with his brother, whom he joined on weekends in New York in binges of drinking and affairs with prostitutes. Despite his failure in the classroom, Eugene did manage to complete several one-act plays, including *Abortion*, which portrayed his view of Ivy League college life.

LOW-LIFE YEARS

After he left Princeton, O'Neill struggled to find a direction in life. He worked as a clerk in a mail-order jewelry house in New York City; patronized radical bookstores and cafés in Greenwich Village; took up with prostitutes; drank heavily in taverns; read philosophy, particularly the works of Nietzsche; shared a studio with the painter George Bellows; and, at times, attended societal supper parties. It was at one of these society affairs that O'Neill met his first wife, Kathleen Jenkins, a debutante who was fascinated by the poetic O'Neill. When he learned of the relationship, a furious James O'Neill accused Kathleen, a Protestant, of wanting only the money that he had amassed through his acting and real-estate investments. In an attempt to end the affair, James arranged for Eugene to sail to Honduras with an engineer who was going to prospect for gold. Two weeks before he left in 1909, at the age of twenty, Eugene secretly married Kathleen, who was pregnant at the time.

During an unproductive and backbreaking expedition in the jungles of Honduras, O'Neill contracted malaria and was shipped back to New York. Upon his return, his father initiated Eugene's divorce and arranged for his son to work with him in the theater as a stage manager. The uncontested divorce became final in 1912; Eugene never saw Kathleen again and did not acknowledge his first son, Eugene Gladstone O'Neill Jr., born on May 6, 1910, until the boy was twelve. Throughout his correspondence, however, O'Neill spoke respectfully about Kathleen, writing once later in life "that the woman I gave the most trouble to has given me the least."

Unhappy working with his father in the theater, Eugene sought escape by signing on with a Norwegian ship that set sail for Buenos Aires. O'Neill found the sea and the sailor's life appealing, but his stay in Buenos Aires was short-lived and he returned to New York broke and aimless. For a year after his return, O'Neill lived in a sleazy New York waterfront saloon–rooming house called Jimmy the Priest's. O'Neill referred to Jimmy the Priest's as a hellhole that was "almost coming down and the principal house wreckers were vermin." The waterfront was populated by a wide array of drifters, seamen, and artists, some of whom found their way into the characters of *The Iceman Cometh* and *Anna Christie.* Despondent about his destitute life and his broken marriage, O'Neill attempted suicide with an overdose of sleeping pills. Only the quick action of some friends prevented his death.

In December 1912, O'Neill, whose health had been tested by hard drinking and a dissolute lifestyle, learned that he had tuberculosis. On Christmas Eve O'Neill entered Gaylord Farm sanatorium at Wallingford, Connecticut, in order to recover physically and regain control of his life. While he was convalescing, O'Neill found the motivation to express his feelings about life—he began to write. His stay at the sanatorium marked a turning point for the playwright:

> It was at Gaylord that my mind got the chance to establish itself, to digest, and evaluate the impressions of many past years in which one experience had crowded on another with never a second's reflection. At Gaylord I really thought about my life for the first time, about past and future.

After six months at Gaylord, O'Neill was well enough to return to his parents' home in New London, where he spent a full summer reading and writing sketches for future work. By the fall of 1914, O'Neill had written several short works including *Bound East for Cardiff.* He wrote that in this seminal play "can be seen, or felt, the germ of the spirit, life-attitude, etc., of all my more important future work." In an attempt to polish his writing as a dramatist, O'Neill enrolled in a dramatic composition workshop at Harvard. Here the young writer's avowed goal was to become "an artist or nothing." Although O'Neill stated that he did not learn much about the theater from George Pierce Baker, the teacher of the workshop, he gained confidence in his ability to write. O'Neill decided not to return to Harvard the following year; instead, he moved back to Greenwich Village in New York. Mingling with artists and intellectuals in ramshackle bars, O'Neill was introduced to the radical thinker George Cram Cook, who with his wife, playwright Susan Glaspell, organized and directed the Cape Cod summer theater productions at the Wharf Theater, Provincetown, Massachusetts. Under the inspiring leadership of Cook, the company of actors at the Wharf Theater, known as the Provincetown Players, produced *Bound East for Cardiff.*

At Provincetown, O'Neill poured his energy into writing full-length plays. He received his first major critical acclaim when in 1917 and in 1918 the plays *The Long Voyage Home, Ile,* and *The Moon of the Caribbees* were published in the *Smart Set* by prominent critic and editor George Jean Nathan. It was through Nathan and his friend and colleague H.L. Mencken that O'Neill was able to sell his three-act tragedy *Beyond the Horizon* and other plays to producers on New York's Broadway. *Beyond the Horizon* was produced by John D. Williams at the Morosco Theater in 1920, first in trials as a matinee and then, when it proved popular, as a featured production that enjoyed a run of more than a hundred performances. The play won the Pulitzer Prize and O'Neill drew widespread attention as a playwright.

O'NEILL AND AGNES BOULTON

In the fall and winter months after the theater season at Provincetown, O'Neill returned to his cronies and the saloons of Greenwich Village. At his favorite drinking place, the Golden Swan Bar, nicknamed the Hell Hole, O'Neill met the writer Agnes Boulton. O'Neill was immediately taken with Agnes; after a night of conversation he told her, "I want to spend every night of my life from now on with you." Not long after, Agnes and O'Neill moved in together in Provincetown along with O'Neill's brother, Jamie. Agnes and Eugene were married on April 12, 1918, and moved that year to Agnes's seaside house in New Jersey. Agnes's family—her daughter by a previous marriage, her sisters, and her parents—had recently moved into the house but were forced to leave when Agnes and Eugene arrived because O'Neill did not want to be bothered while he wrote. But Agnes was unhappy in the drafty old house, so they soon moved back to Provincetown and settled in a remodeled Coast Guard station purchased for them as a gift by James O'Neill. Their son, Shane Rudraighe O'Neill, was born in 1919, and a daughter, Oona, was born in 1925.

In 1920 James O'Neill died of cancer. Jamie, unemployed and living at home with his mother, helped settle his father's debts and investments. In California with Jamie to sell some orange groves that James had purchased, Ella fell sick and died quickly in a hospital. Jamie, shaken terribly by the loss, tried to find comfort in drink. At age forty-two he was a confirmed alcoholic who moved in and out of sanatoriums for a year and a half after Ella's death in a futile attempt to overcome his addiction. Although he possessed a keen sense of humor and a fine intellect, Jamie's life was unstable and, by all accounts, unsuccessful. He initially attempted to follow his father into acting, but his heart was not in it and he was relegated to bit parts in insignificant plays. Apparently unable to shake a listless and indifferent attitude, he repeatedly lapsed into heavy drinking and meaningless affairs with women he met in and around the theater. Suffering from delirium tremens, Jamie died from complications of alcoholism in 1923. In just three years, Eugene had lost his mother, father, and older brother. Grief-stricken by the death of Jamie, whom he deeply loved, Eugene went on a drinking binge himself and missed his brother's funeral. Years later, in a letter to a friend, O'Neill wrote that Jamie "never found his place. He had never belonged."

Despite these losses, the period with Agnes from 1918 to 1928 were years of significant output for O'Neill. Soon after his father died, O'Neill wrote the initial draft of *Anna Christie* and he completed *The Emperor Jones* and *Diff'rent.* The success of these plays improved O'Neill's financial situation dramatically. Both *The Emperor Jones* and *The Hairy Ape*, which O'Neill wrote in three weeks during 1921, were first staged with the Provincetown Players and then moved to Broadway. Despite recurring bouts of alcoholism, the deaths of his mother and brother, and ongoing turmoil with Agnes, O'Neill enjoyed one theatrical success after another. His second Pulitzer Prize–winning play, *Anna Christie*, opened to rave reviews in London; the Provincetown Playhouse produced *All God's Chillun Got Wings;* the Greenwich Village Theatre staged *Desire Under the Elms* in 1924 and *The Great God Brown* in 1926; and on Broadway O'Neill won some of his greatest acclaim for productions of *Marco Millions*, in 1927, and *Strange Interlude*, which was awarded the playwright's third Pulitzer Prize in 1928.

As O'Neill's success as a dramatist steadily grew, his relationship with Agnes became increasingly hostile, particularly when he was drunk. O'Neill claimed that Agnes's desire to continue writing short stories and her inept housekeeping interfered with his proficiency as a playwright. At one point, in frustration and outrage, O'Neill built a little wooden shack on the edge of their property to get away from the noise and "smell of dirty diapers." Ultimately, the dramatist decided that he needed warm weather, the sea, and an out-of-the-way place to work. During the winter of 1925 he moved his family to Bermuda, where he bought a two-hundred-year-old spacious estate called Spithead. O'Neill boasted that "the place will be a wonder when it's fixed up," but he found little tranquillity there. He fought with Agnes, complaining about the remodelers, and fretted over interruptions to his writing. With the approach of summer, the O'Neills returned to their lodge in Maine, where the playwright met a beautiful actress, Carlotta Monterey, who was vacationing nearby with a friend.

Dissatisfied with his marriage and family obligations, O'Neill spent more and more time with Carlotta, who coincidentally had played Mildred in a Broadway production of *The Hairy Ape*. By Christmas 1927, O'Neill wrote to Agnes telling her that he had fallen in love with Carlotta and that they should maintain separate lives. Finally, in 1929, after many heated exchanges, Agnes agreed to a proposed financial settlement and went to Reno for a divorce on the grounds of desertion. At that point Agnes dropped out of O'Neill's life, but in 1958 she wrote a memoir of their time together, entitled *Part of a Long Story*, which portrays O'Neill as abusive and prone to explosive fits of rage. O'Neill's relationship with his children Shane and Oona was spotty, tenuously maintained through occasional letters and infrequent visits.

O'NEILL'S CHILDREN

Eugene O'Neill inflicted many of the same parental inadequacies on his children that he himself endured as James and Ella's son. He had always required long periods of uninterrupted and quiet time to write. Generally, O'Neill wrote from early morning to midafternoon, after which he scheduled time for solitary exercise like walking or swimming. O'Neill's art came first, his family a distant second at best.

O'Neill did not see his first son, Eugene Jr., born in 1910, until 1922. Kathleen Jenkins O'Neill never asked for child support and reared the boy with her second husband, who by all accounts was a decent stepfather. Eugene Jr., renamed Richard Pitt-Smith after his mother's remarriage, spent the early years of his education in a military school, where he was as unhappy as his biological father had been in boarding school. In an attempt to secure financial assistance for his education, Eugene Jr.'s maternal grandmother made arrangements for the boy to meet O'Neill. Eugene Jr. was handsome, charming, and bright and almost immediately a respectful friendship grew between father and son. O'Neill helped finance his son's education at Yale, where in 1936 Eugene Jr. earned a doctorate in classics. Although he gained a reputation as an expert in his field, Eugene Jr.'s life gradually deteriorated during three bad marriages, habitual heavy drinking, and a faltering career. At age forty, he committed suicide by slashing his wrists in a bathtub. Weighted down by an empty bottle of bourbon, his suicide note read in part, "Never let it be said of O'Neill that he failed to finish a bottle."

O'Neill's second son, Shane, born to Agnes Boulton, was a quiet, sensitive, and lonely child. A close friend of the O'Neills, Eben Given, stated that she "hardly ever saw Gene play with Shane. . . . He seemed detached from the boy." After O'Neill left Agnes for Carlotta Monterey, Shane was shuffled among a series of boarding schools, where the unhappy boy got into trouble and scored low grades. His adult life was a desperate mix of unsuccessful attempts at writing; three unhappy marriages; heroin, Benzedrine, and alcohol abuse; the death of his first child apparently to Sudden Infant Death Syndrome; several arrests for disorderly behavior; and numerous suicide attempts. Finally, in 1977 Shane jumped to his death from a fourteenth-floor apartment building window.

O'Neill saw little of his third child, Oona, since Agnes and Eugene divorced when their daughter was only four years old. As a teenager, forgoing a chance to attend Vassar, Oona went to Hollywood to find acting work. There she met the movie star Charles Chaplin, whom she married in 1943 when she was eighteen and Chaplin was fifty-four, the same age as her father. The marriage outraged O'Neill and he never spoke to Oona again. Oona and Chaplin moved to Switzerland, enjoyed a stable marriage, and raised eight children, apparently escaping the family dysfunction that destroyed Eugene Jr. and Shane.

Although O'Neill claimed in many of his letters to love his children intensely, his behavior indicated that his claim might have been more obligatory than genuine. In a letter to his friend Kenneth Macgowan in 1926, O'Neill admitted, "I was never cut out, seemingly, for a pater familias and children in squads, even when indubitably my own, tend to 'get my goat.'" When O'Neill's will was read after his death in 1953, Shane and Oona discovered that they had both been purposely excluded from their father's estate.

O'NEILL AND CARLOTTA MONTEREY

O'Neill's third wife, Carlotta Monterey, was a beautiful, manipulative actress whose acting success was based more on her dark, exotic beauty than her talent. Her nickname was "the Swan" because she had a long, graceful neck that reminded her friends of the Egyptian queen Cleopatra. Carlotta had ended three marriages and, just prior to meeting O'Neill, a six-year affair with a wealthy Wall Street banker named James Speyer. Shortly before she committed to O'Neill, she arranged to have approximately $14,000 a year for life sent to her via a trust fund set up by Speyer. O'Neill never realized that the money came from a former lover. With a previous husband, Carlotta had a daughter, Cynthia, who was sent to boarding school at an early age and had very little contact with her mother. Early in their relationship, Carlotta and Eugene traveled throughout Europe and the Orient searching for a perfect place to settle. O'Neill's heavy drinking and their tempestuous personalities led to some vicious bickering, but eventually their distinct roles in the union began to emerge. The playwright sought absolute privacy in order to write, and Carlotta's role became that of O'Neill's caretaker. She devoted her life to managing O'Neill's affairs, including his correspondence, telephone calls, and visitors. In a sense, with Carlotta as guardian, O'Neill detached himself from the past. Journalists, agents, producers, and old friends had to go through Carlotta to gain access to O'Neill. Carlotta even treated O'Neill's children, particularly Shane and Oona, as outsiders and virtually cut them off from their father for long periods of time.

The couple's relationship was marred by disputes and bitter accusations, punctuated by periods of separation, and defined by bouts of physical collapse and emotional loneliness. Carlotta insisted that "there was no mad love affair between us. O'Neill was a tough mick and never loved a woman who walked. He loved only his work." Loyal nonetheless, while he was writing, Carlotta gave him the structure, organization, and orderliness that he demanded.

With Carlotta managing the details of his life, O'Neill became immersed in his writing. His work habits were seemingly indefatigable. In a minuscule longhand, he wrote and rewrote each manuscript many times. While he was writing, everything took second place, even Carlotta. After two years of work, he finished *Mourning Becomes Electra*, and shortly thereafter he wrote *Days Without End* and *Ah, Wilderness!* The latter, a rare comedy, was produced by the Theatre Guild and had an exciting and successful run in 1933. After pushing himself very hard for a long period of time, O'Neill and Carlotta, aiming to regain the playwright's strength, rented a house in Seattle overlooking Puget Sound. While they were there, O'Neill learned that he had been awarded the Nobel Prize for literature for 1936. Ill and publicity shy, the playwright did not attend the ceremony and, after moving to San Francisco to avoid notoriety, he was hospitalized for an appendectomy.

With the $40,000 cash award that accompanied the Nobel Prize, Eugene and Carlotta built a Chinese-style house, called Tao House, on 158 acres in Contra Costa County, California. O'Neill told a friend that "We really have an ideal home with one of the most beautiful views I have seen—pure country with no taint of suburbia, and yet we are only fifty minutes' drive from the heart of San Francisco—my favorite American city, although I don't like any city much." In their new home O'Neill and Carlotta led a secluded and private life. From 1937 to 1943, O'Neill worked on a huge project about the Irish in America that he intended to call *A Tale of Possessors Dispossessed*. After pouring countless hours of work and creative energy into the project, he deemed it to be inadequate and, ultimately, destroyed most of it.

It was during this period that O'Neill isolated himself from the theater establishment and refused to release his plays for production, shunning Broadway and the Theatre Guild. O'Neill did not have a new Broadway production since an unpopular 1934 staging of *Days Without End*, often considered by critics as O'Neill's worst produced play. Nevertheless, he found a creative resurgence in 1939 and ended his writing career with his three family plays, which not only equaled his best previous work but by most accounts surpassed it: *The Iceman Cometh* (1939) recalls his days in New York at Jimmy the Priest's saloon; *Long Day's Journey into Night* (1939–1941), wrestles with the turmoil of his own family; and *A Moon for the Misbegotten* (1941–1943), remembers the last years of his brother, Jamie. Writing *Long Day's Journey into Night* was a great emotional struggle for the playwright. In the play's dedication, he writes that the drama was "written in tears and blood." Since the play was so personal, O'Neill left instructions that it should not be released until twenty-five years after his death. However, just three years after he died, Carlotta released the play to the Royal Dramatic Theatre of Stockholm. Soon the play reached Broadway, where it established O'Neill once again as a dominant force in American theater. *Long Day's Journey into Night* posthumously won him his fourth Pulitzer Prize.

O'Neill had begun to feel the creeping effects of a neurological disease as early as 1936. By 1942 the disorder left him with trembling hands and tremors that shuddered his whole body, making it impossible for O'Neill to write. In a letter to his friend George Jean Nathan, O'Neill talked succinctly about his illness, which had been misdiagnosed as Parkinson's disease: "The old Parkinson's went wild and woolly." Moreover, the relationship between Carlotta and Eugene continued fractious. Perhaps because of poor health, heavy medication, close proximity, or strong wills, the O'Neills quarreled bitterly. At one point, after a hysterical Carlotta was picked up by the police wandering in the snow, O'Neill tried unsuccessfully to have her institutionalized as incompetent. Nevertheless, underneath the rage and the battles, there was a strong dependence on each other. At one point, after a brief separation, O'Neill wrote to Carlotta, "Darling: For the love of God, forgive and come back. You are all I have in life. I am sick and I will surely die without you." Carlotta joined Eugene in Boston at the Hotel Shelton, where he had moved when they had separated. Weak and bedridden, O'Neill spent the last two years of his life in a hotel suite overlooking the Charles River, utterly dependent on Carlotta. In November 1953, at age sixty-five, Eugene O'Neill caught pneumonia, lapsed into a thirty-six-hour coma, and died.

A MISSION TO FIND MEANING

Once while reminiscing, O'Neill talked about a significant turning point in his life at the age of eighteen in 1907. O'Neill met Benjamin Tucker, the owner of a New York bookstore called the Unique Book Shop. Tucker was a fifty-year-old radical who introduced the impressionable O'Neill to the anarchistic ideas of writers like Proudhon, Zola, and Mirabeau. When Tucker gave his protégé a copy of Friedrich Nietzsche's *Thus Spake Zarathustra* O'Neill studied it, absorbed it, and began to build a personal philosophical system modeled on its ideas. In his forties, O'Neill wrote to a critic that this work by the German philosopher "has influenced me more than any book I've ever read . . . and every year or so I re-read it and am never disappointed, which is more than I can say of almost any other book." As a thoughtful young man, O'Neill copied key passages into a notebook and committed them to memory. One quote that O'Neill copied is particularly relevant to his life as a writer: "I am a wanderer and a mountain climber. . . . I like not the plains, and it seemeth I cannot long sit still." In his artistic life O'Neill could not sit still. He challenged himself; he anguished with the struggle to find meaning, love, and the eternal; and he pushed the boundaries of American theater. The novelist Sinclair Lewis recognized O'Neill's achievement when he said that the playwright's role in American drama was "to transform it utterly in ten or twelve years from a false world of neat and competent trickery to a world of splendor, fear and greatness." Like the major characters in his plays, O'Neill was on a mission to find meaning. At times the quest was turbulent and futile, but he never abandoned the struggle.

O'Neill was an artist both liberated by his art and in thrall to it. He translated his personal torment into artistic explorations of the psychological boundaries of the human condition. His plays reached an American audience tired of the surface realism of pre–World War I theater: O'Neill redefined American theater by employing psychological naturalism, sardonic humor, and the moods of tragedy to speak directly to the issues of power, race, family, materialism, adultery, fate, and psychic identity. As an artist, O'Neill was a mountain climber.

CHAPTER 1

Introduction to the Playwright

O'Neill's Relationship to the Theater

Egil Törnqvist

During O'Neill's youth American theater was dominated by sentimental and melodramatic plays catering to mass tastes. Egil Törnqvist reports that O'Neill revolted against commercialism and looked to more serious European drama for inspiration. According to Törnqvist, O'Neill's attitude toward the established theatrical world was always characterized by ambivalence and disillusionment. Often weary of actors, rehearsals, and productions, he felt that staged versions of his plays could not equal the imaginative power of his written work. Törnqvist concludes that O'Neill wrote for both a reading and a viewing audience.

Egil Törnqvist is a professor of Scandinavian studies at the University of Amsterdam. He is the author of *Between Stage and Screen: Ingmar Bergman Directs, Ibsen's "A Doll's House": Plays in Production,* and *Transposing Drama: Studies in Representation; New Directions in Theatre.*

The whole period from O'Neill's birth in 1888 to his debut in 1914 was marked by the commercialization of the American theatre. In 1896 the first Theatrical Syndicate was formed, and despite the opposition from a number of producers and actors, James O'Neill [Eugene's father] being one of them, it had within ten years gained control over most theatres in the country. The repertoire was dominated by light entertainment, sentimental and sensational pieces. Playwriting meant adjustment to what the masses desired. The playwright's main task was to learn the tricks of the trade by which he could allure his audience. There was no native tradition to boast of, and even the best American dramatists of the time—men like William Moody, James Herne and Clyde Fitch—seemed rather mediocre when compared to their European contemporaries: Ibsen, Strindberg, Maeterlinck, Hauptmann, Wedekind, Schnitzler, Chekhov, Shaw and Synge. Not only did Europe have much more to offer in the way of serious drama, but ever since the foundation of the Théâtre Libre in 1887 it also had a number of experimental theatres where this drama could be staged.

O'NEILL'S VIEW OF TRADITIONAL AMERICAN THEATRE

There was obviously little in the American theatre that could appeal to the young O'Neill. "My early experience with the theatre through my father," he once said, "really made me revolt against it." And he added: "As a boy I saw so much of the old, ranting, artificial romantic stuff that I always had a sort of contempt for the theatre." It is difficult to ascertain to what extent O'Neill's revolt was a revolt against the conventional theatre and to what extent it was a rebellion against the father who was associated with it. The dramatist himself once pointed out that he found it "perfectly natural that having been brought up around the old conventional theatre, and having identified it with my father, I should rebel and go in a new direction." In a letter to the *New York Times*, composed at the death of Professor George Pierce Baker and published on January 13, 1935, O'Neill summed up his impressions of the American theatre at the time of his debut as follows:

> Only those of us who had the privilege in the drama class of George Pierce Baker back in the dark age when the American theatre was still, for playwrights, the closed shop, star system, amusement racket, can know what a profound influence Professor Baker . . . exerted toward the encouragement and birth of modern American drama.

> It is difficult in these days, when the native playwright can function in comparative freedom, to realize that in that benighted period a play of any imagination, originality or integrity by an American was almost automatically barred from a hearing in our theatre. To write plays of life as one saw and felt it, instead of concocting the conventional theatrical drivel of the time, seemed utterly hopeless.

Whatever O'Neill learned from this artificial and traditional type of theatre was a negative knowledge; "it helped me," he once said, "because I knew what I wanted to *avoid* doing."

A more varied view he held with regard to the American theatre of the twenties and thirties. Occasionally he would take a rather favorable attitude to it. At other times he would be as negative about it as about the Broadway of his youth. Thus in 1925 he contemptuously characterized the contemporary (American) theatre as "a realtor's medium" and pessimistically viewed an artistic theatre as "an unrealizable dream.". . . It was apparently the acquaintance with modern European drama that opened O'Neill's eyes to his own possibilities. In 1907 the nineteen-year-old boy saw Alla Nazimova's troupe in *Hedda Gabler* "for ten successive nights": "That experience discovered an entire new world of the drama for me. It gave me my first conception of a modern theatre where truth might live." Four years later he saw the Irish players doing Yeats, Synge and Lady Gregory: "It was seeing the Irish players for the first time that gave me a glimpse of my opportunity. The first year that they came over here I went to see everything they did." Two years after this event he discovered [Swedish playwright, August] Strindberg:

> It was reading his plays when I first started to write back in the winter of 1913–14 that, above all else, first gave me the vision of what modern drama could be, and first inspired me with the urge to write for the theatre myself. If there is anything of lasting worth in my work, it is due to that original impulse from him, which has continued as my inspiration down all the years since then—to the ambition I received then to follow in the footsteps of his genius as worthily as my talent might permit, and with the same integrity of purpose.

Feeling the need "to study the technique of play-writing," O'Neill in 1914–15 attended George Pierce Baker's famous 47 Workshop, a course in playwriting and play production. As his tribute to Baker indicates, O'Neill respected the man more than the teacher. Most of what Baker had to tell his students about the theatre as a physical medium was "old stuff" to O'Neill. What he learned from the course was mainly a practical work method. "Without the shortcut of your advice," he wrote Baker in 1919, "I would have learned (if I have learned!) by a laborious process of elimination." Aside from this, Baker's importance, as O'Neill made plain in his letter to the *Times*, consisted chiefly in the encouragement he gave his students that a new era would dawn in which the serious playwright would get a hearing in the theatre.

O'NEILL AND THE PROVINCETOWN PLAYERS

Of greater importance was O'Neill's connection with the Provincetown Players. This group, which consisted of some radical intellectuals and artists—novelists, journalists, sculptors, teachers, architects—who spent their summers in Provincetown, Massachusetts, began its activities very modestly at about the time when O'Neill left Baker's course. When he arrived in the little fishing village in the summer of 1916, apparently in the hope of getting one of his sixteen plays produced, he was immediately recognized as a dramatist of stature; and, ironically, he won his recognition almost solely on the basis of the play Professor Baker had thought no play at all. "So Gene took 'Bound East for Cardiff' from his trunk," Susan Glaspell has recalled, "and Freddie Burt read it to us. . . . Then we knew what we were for." The play was produced the same summer in what was by this time called "The Wharf Theater," a deserted old shed for fishing gear and boat repair. The production marked not only the first staging of an O'Neill play but also the beginning of a new era in the American theatre, an era characterized by greater sincerity and integrity.

It is likely that the Provincetown Players would have continued their activities even without O'Neill. And O'Neill, for his part, has stated that he would have gone on writing plays even without the Players. Yet it is obvious—and acknowledged by both parties—that each benefited enormously from the other. . . . Precisely because the members of the group were not professionally engaged in the theatre, they had no prejudices about plays or play production. In the manifesto, drawn up on September 5, 1916, it was stated that the primary object of the Provincetown Players was

> to encourage the writing of American plays of artistic, literary and dramatic—as opposed to Broadway—merit.
>
> That such plays be considered without reference to their commercial value, since this theatre is not to be run for pecuniary profit. . . .
>
> That the president shall cooperate with the author in producing the play under the author's direction. The resources of the theatre . . . shall be placed at the disposal of the author. . . . The author shall produce the play without hindrance, according to his own ideas.

Thinking perhaps of Strindberg's Intimate Theatre, O'Neill suggested that the group name their theatre on Macdougal Street in New York "The Playwright's Theatre." Nevertheless, he seems from the very first to have been relatively disinterested in the production of his own plays.

Although, as we have seen, the Players granted the playwright the right to supervise the staging of his plays, O'Neill would leave most of this work to George Cram Cook, despite the fact that "he was not always in agreement with 'Jig's' ideas." [O'Neill's biographers] report that O'Neill would "reluctantly" agree to supervise the staging of *Cardiff* in New York. Since this is a play which O'Neill valued highly, and since it meant the first production of an O'Neill play in New York, this reluctance is surprising.

Agnes Boulton recalls that O'Neill would become moody when he was expected to attend rehearsals of *Caribbees:* "He really wanted to settle down to work on his plays. At times he even tried to persuade himself and me that it would be just as well if he attended only the last rehearsal or so and left the rest of it up to Jig Cook." Finally, because *Caribbees* was his favorite play and because Cook had no time for it, O'Neill resigned himself to attending rehearsals, but apparently without any enthusiasm; less than a month after the play opened he complained about the production and could not even remember the name of the director. O'Neill once told Nina Moise, who directed *Rope:* "When I finish writing a play, I'm through with it." And Moise, in line with this, has observed that "Gene was concerned with plays, not theatre."

O'Neill and Play Production

While attending rehearsals of *Horizon* O'Neill wrote his wife Agnes: "I'd never go near a rehearsal if I didn't have to—and I'll certainly never see a performance." In 1929 he told Eleanor Fitzgerald: "I'm a bit weary and disillusioned with scenery and actors. . . . I sigh for the old P'town days, the old crowd and zest. . . . I think I will wind up writing plays to be published with 'No Productions Allowed' in red letters on the first page." The twelve-year absence of a new O'Neill play from Broadway (1934–46) his wife Carlotta has partly explained as due to the dramatist's dislike of attending rehearsals: "The only thing he cared about was his writing. He used to say, 'Oh, God, if only some Good Fairy would give me some money, so I'd never have to produce a play, and I could just write, write, write and never go near a theatre!' ". . .

He might have added that seeing a play of his own was a painful experience for him also because of the discrepancy between the production he had done in his mind as he wrote

the play and the one executed on the stage. O'Neill frequently drew attention to this aspect. While attending rehearsals
of *Horizon* he complained: "Those people will never—can
never—be my Robert, Ruth, and Andy—and what would be
the use of my watching another lot of actors perform—after
all these years of watching them?" By 1929 he had seen no
performance which fully realized his intentions: "I've had
many plays in which the acting was excellent. I've never had
one I recognized on the stage as being deeply my play. That's
why I never see them.". . .

O'Neill's disappointment with most actors is partly due to
the high standard of acting he demanded. But more important is the fact that he felt unusually close to his characters:
"I've always tried to *write* my characters out. That's why I've
sometimes been disappointed in the actors who played
them—the characters were too real and alive in my imagination." As is now well known, many of the characters are
intimately autobiographical; presumably O'Neill found it
especially hard to accept the actors' interpretations of parts
into which he had written a good deal of himself, his parents, his brother or his wives.

WRITTEN PLAYS COMPARED WITH STAGED PRODUCTIONS

To O'Neill the staged version of a great play could never equal
the written one. Even a perfect and imaginative production
would have the limiting boundaries inherent in a physical
production as compared to a purely imagined one. It would
also lack the unity found in the written play, being the product of but one mind: "After all, is not the written play a thing?
Is not *Hamlet*, seen in the dream theatre of the imagination
as one reads, a greater play than *Hamlet* interpreted even by
a perfect production?" O'Neill, the avid play reader who
never went to the theatre and who attended rehearsals of his
own plays mainly to prevent his work from being misinter-
preted, obviously thought so. In 1929 he wrote [critic
Benjamin] De Casseres: "A play's fate after I have written it—
—I mean outside of my creation, the play in the book—is just
roulette to me with a fat percentage in favor of the author losing *his* play either artistically or financially or both.". . .

Considering the author's high evaluation of the written
play, it is not surprising that the epic or novelistic trend
should be rather marked in his work. When outlining
Horizon, O'Neill revealed in a letter to the *New York Times*,

he "dreamed of wedding the theme for a novel to the play form in a way that would still leave the play master of the house." He characterized *Chris* as an attempt "to compress the theme for a novel into play form without losing the flavor of the novel." In *Interlude* with its long time span and its constant thought asides the novelistic tendency is very evident. About the plays in the projected series *By Way of Obit*, of which only *Hughie* was completed, O'Neill told Nathan that they were written "more to be read than staged, although they could be played." The ample, descriptive stage directions, to which the dramatist appears to have devoted as much attention as to the dialogue, give an epic touch to all O'Neill's plays, as does the unusual length of some of them. From one point of view this tendency may be regarded as an attempt to overcome the limitations inherent in the dramatic form. From another, relevant in this context, it may be said to constitute an attempt to give artistic confirmation of O'Neill's view that the written play is the thing.

O'NEILL'S IDEAL THEATRE

Yet it would clearly be absurd to argue that O'Neill wrote solely for the reader. Despite his skeptical attitude to the theatre of his day, O'Neill never wrote a closet drama and he was clearly interested in having his plays produced; in 1926 he even nourished plans for an O'Neill repertory theatre. Many of the effects in the plays are also of a strongly theatrical nature.

Moreover, there are statements by the author which support the view that O'Neill wrote also, perhaps preeminently, for the physical theatre—if not for the one of his time. In the wake of [German philosopher Friedrich] Nietzsche he dreamt of an ennobled theatre, filled with artists of a higher order than the ones he saw crowding the New York stages; in 1921 he told an interviewer:

> Yes, I can almost hear the birth cry of the Higher Man in the theatre. There is a goal, blessedly difficult of attainment. And what will he be? . . . Well, the Higher Man of the theatre will be a playwright, say. He will have his own theatre for his own plays, as Strindberg had his Intimate Theatre in Stockholm. He will have grouped around him as fellow workers in that theatre the most imaginative of all the artists in the different crafts. In no sense will he be their master, except his imagination of his work will be the director of their imaginations. He will tell them the inner meaning and spiritual signifi-

cance of his play as revealed to him. He will explain the truth—the unity—underlying his conception. And then all will work together to express that unity. The playwright will not interfere except where he sees the harmony of his imaginative whole is threatened. Rather, he will learn from his associates, help them to set their imaginations free as they help to find in the actual theatre a medium ever-broadening in which even his seventh last solitude may hope to speak and be interpreted. And soon all of these would be Higher Men of the theatre.

It was for such a theatre, it might be held, that most of O'Neill's plays were written, a theatre which he hoped would be "the theatre of tomorrow." And it was presumably this kind of theatre he had in mind when he subtitled *Lazarus "A Play for an Imaginative Theatre."* In his letter to the Kamerny Theatre, whose production of *Chillun* impressed him, O'Neill stated: "A theatre of creative imagination has always been my ideal! To see my plays given by such a theatre has always been my dream!"

Along with George Cram Cook and Kenneth Macgowan O'Neill, the renegade Catholic, dreamt of the theatre as a "Living Church," the one 'church' left to modern man after "the death of the old God and the failure of science and materialism to give any satisfying new one." In an unpublished "Author's foreword" to *Brown* he states: "The theatre should stand as apart from existence as the church did in the days when it was the church. It should give us what the church no longer gives us—a meaning. In brief, it should return to the spirit of the Greek grandeur.". . .

It would appear, then, that O'Neill, hostile towards the physical theatre of his day, wrote both for what he himself termed "the dream theatre," i.e. the theatre of the mind, and for an "emotionally charged" imaginative theatre of the future, hence for two audiences: a reading and a viewing audience. Since he never published any of the original acting versions, we must assume that he meant the published plays to function not merely as reading matter but also as texts for future productions. And even of the passages that seem directed primarily to the general reader we cannot feel sure that they are not meant as much for the actor and director. Thus, when O'Neill has Murray in *Straw* clench his fists *"in impotent rage at himself and at Fate"* or assures us that *"for the first time Death confronts him* [Murray] *face to face as a menacing reality,"* when he has the Cabot brothers in *Desire* "*smell of earth*," or when he has Margaret in *Brown* kiss "*with a timeless kiss*" and Cybel in the same play chew gum "*like a sacred cow forgetting time with an eternal end,*" he is, I believe, doing two things at the same time. He is explaining the significance of the characters' actions to the *reader* to help him do a better production in his mind. And he is providing "road signs for the intelligent actor" to help him do a better production for the *spectator.* To what extent we consider stage directions such as these primarily meant for the general reader or for the actor and thus, indirectly, for the spectator, depends on to what extent we consider them realizable in the theatre.

A Critical Assessment

Oscar Cargill, N. Bryllion Fagin, and
William J. Fisher

In the introduction to their book *O'Neill and His Plays,* editors Oscar Cargill, N. Bryllion Fagin, and William J. Fisher write that O'Neill's importance to American theater remains hotly contested by the critics. Because O'Neill's works are experimental and provocative they are either lauded or hated by the critics. The authors of the article excerpted here suggest that the playwright has been enthusiastically and warmly received by European critics who hail O'Neill as the voice of America.

Oscar Cargill is a critic of American literature and the head of the All-University Department of English at New York University. N. Bryllion Fagin is professor emeritus of English at Johns Hopkins University and the director of the Johns Hopkins Playshop. William J. Fisher is a professor of English at Rutgers University and a Fulbright lecturer at the University of Delhi, India.

The death of Eugene O'Neill on November 27, 1953, served as an occasion for critical evaluations and revaluations of the work of America's most eminent dramatist. He had been sick for many years, and the last play he had offered to the theatre world was *The Iceman Cometh,* produced in 1946 but written in 1939. In our hectic age, when dramatic reputations flare up one night and sputter out at the end of a week, seven years of silence remove an author into prehistory. O'Neill, when he died, was a forgotten man, or remembered only by literary historians, academicians, and an older generation of drama critics as someone who had once started a revolution in the theatre—a revolution which proved only partially victorious—had been rewarded with three Pulitzer awards and a Nobel Prize, and then was heard from no more.

Excerpted from the editor's Introduction to *O'Neill and His Plays: Four Decades of Criticism,* edited by Oscar Cargill, N. Bryllion Fagin, and William J. Fisher (New York: New York University Press, 1961). Copyright © New York University. Reprinted by permission of the publisher.

It is significant that almost all the articles—whether editorial, critical, or "scholarly"—which the daily press and the weekly, monthly, and quarterly periodicals throughout the world printed on the occasion of his death displayed a tone of partisanship. They were either aggressively laudatory or violently antagonistic; few were "balanced." It looked as if the fire and violence which characterized O'Neill's plays had carried over into the mood of his critics: the revolution was still on and O'Neill was not dead at all.

O'NEILL'S COMMITMENT TO HIS ART

In a June 1920 letter to drama critic George Jean Nathan published in the Boston Evening Postscript *and reprinted in* O'Neill and His Plays: Four Decades of Criticism *by Oscar Cargill, N. Bryllion Fagin, and William J. Fisher, aspiring playwright Eugene O'Neill pledges that he will continue to struggle, experiment, and grow as a writer.*

I am familiar enough with the best modern drama of all countries to realize that, viewed from a true standard, my work is as yet a mere groping. I rate myself as a beginner—with prospects. I acknowledge that when you write: "He sees life too often as drama. The great dramatist is the dramatist who sees drama as life," you are smiting the nail on the head. But I venture to promise that this will be less true with each succeeding play—that I will not "stay put" in any comfortable niche and play the leave-well-enough-alone game. God stiffen it, I am young yet and I mean to grow! And in this faith I live: That if I have the "guts" to ignore the megaphone men and what goes with them, to follow the dream and live for that alone, then my real significant bit of truth, and the ability to express it, will be conquered in time—not tomorrow nor the next day nor any near, easily-attained period, but after the struggle has been long enough and hard enough to merit victory.

As, indeed, he was not. Three years after his corporeal death, a play of his, written in 1940 but never produced or published, was given to the world by his widow, and it exploded as most of his plays, beginning with his early one-acters of the sea, had exploded during his lifetime. *Long Day's Journey into Night* brought him the plaudits of a new generation of theatregoers and drama critics wherever it was presented, whether in Stockholm, where it was first unveiled on the stage of the Royal Dramatic Theatre on the evening of February 10, 1955, or in New York, where it induced the Pulitzer judges for 1956 to bestow a posthumous prize upon its author, or in London, where it impressed another Nobel Prize winner, T. S. Eliot, as "one of the most moving plays" he had ever seen. Everywhere it led to the revival of other plays by O'Neill, and in New York it also led to the naming of a theatre in his honor.

O'NEILL AND CONTROVERSY

But the battle of the critics over the importance of O'Neill's contribution to American drama or to drama in general is not, however, over, and is not likely to be for some decades to come, if ever. O'Neill remains a controversial writer, a subject guaranteed to raise the blood pressure of contestants, and it would seem that everyone who has an opinion on O'Neill—whether professional critic, college professor, college student, or merely theatre patron—is a contestant. After the television version of *The Iceman Cometh* was shown in Baltimore on April 8, 1961, a new type of theatre public expressed its judgment; dozens of viewers wrote to their local newspapers either to praise or to damn the play, its sponsors, and the channel that made it available to the public. The veteran critic on the *Baltimore Sun,* Donald Kirkley, who had seen the original production on the stage fourteen years before, thought that the drama had grown in stature and that it was "a somber, terrifying masterwork," but many of his readers differed with him violently, just as violently as those who agreed with him.

The plays of O'Neill, it seems, touch something fundamental in those who expose themselves to their effect. They reach down to frightening depths; they step on private, social, religious, philosophical, aesthetic toes; they either evoke immoderate enthusiasm or provoke immoderate anger. Almost every one of his plays has produced warring factions, whose representatives have often been led to express themselves in dogmatic or categorical terms. In the January 1960 issue of *Theatre Arts* Louis Kronenberger summarized the achievements of American playwriting in the preceding decade and came to the conclusion that *Long Day's Journey* was "the great event in the American theatre of the '50's." He characterized the play as "overwhelming drama, something with all the thrust of great theatre and all the convincingness of life." But, writing in the same year,

William L. Sharp, a university theatre director, lamented that "The popularity of Eugene O'Neill who can't write at all" attests "to the insensitive ear not only of the playwright and his audience, but the dramatic critic as well" (*Tulane Drama Review*, Winter, 1960). And, to add a later entry— and, incidentally, to indicate that the battle is global— Günther Crack, reviewing a performance of *Strange Interlude* in Berlin, exclaims that "This play could only have been written by O'Neill, who combined great theatrical talent with an enormous knowledge of the human soul" (*Cultural News from Germany*, April 1961).

O'NEILL'S STATUS AS A PLAYWRIGHT

Perhaps it is too early to assign O'Neill a definite place in the history of dramatic writing. Certainly it is too soon after his death to do so, for in the case of writers who achieve great popularity and critical acclaim during their lifetime there is usually a sudden rush to downgrade them the moment their death is announced. . . . It is as if the critics had been waiting for the celebrity to leave the room before they could say all the things they have resented about him.

And there is generally much to resent. Fame itself, like prosperity in general, tends to arouse resentment, secret and uncrystallized at first, in time open and articulate. In addition, critics, being but human, are subject to the mutability which shadows love affairs. By the time a famous writer is ready to die, some of his admirers have fallen in love with a new face, figure, image, voice, gesture. The newcomer may not fulfill his promise, but only time can test the durability of a lover or a writer. There is also, especially for younger critics, the problem of a Cause to fight for. Writers whose work is nonconformist or contains a shock to, or challenge of, the conventions can easily become a Cause. In the Twenties O'Neill was a Cause, as were Ibsen, Hauptmann, Verhaeren, Shaw, Brieux, and Andreyev before him. Sometimes a writer, if his "message," style, or shock of recognition is strong enough, becomes a Cause for a generation not his own—Chekhov, Brecht, Strindberg, Ghelderode. Complex sociological and psychological factors are involved. But, generally, time winnows greatness; distance provides comparison; emotions cool and judgment becomes balanced. Perhaps it was this process that Friedrich Duerrenmatt had in mind when he remarked, in an interview, "We are too close to him [O'Neill] now to appreciate him fully, but he will continue to grow" (*The New York Times*, May 25, 1958). O'Neill is apparently one of those writers who are destined to have more than one life. After a period of denigration they are rediscovered and reinstated in esteem, or a new generation discovers them for the first time and finds them important. All signs indicate that he will not have to wait as long as, for example, Georg Büchner has had to wait.

[In considering] O'Neill and his plays—their meaning, value, strengths, and weaknesses—other subjects emerge. One is the old question of whether absolutely objective dramatic criticism, or any kind of criticism, is possible. It seems clear once again that criticism can be only relatively objective, especially when it is competent, for then it partakes of the creative act, and all creative expression involves a commitment to a point of view, an orientation, and a strategy which, in turn, involves selection, organization, suppression, and stress—in other words, subtle participation as man and writer. A play is not only what it is but what it does to and for the critic, and what it does depends upon who he is and in what intellectual and aesthetic ambiance he moves. . . .

After *Anna Christie* O'Neill can be said to have done with rigid realism or naturalism—except for a play of recollection such as *Ah, Wilderness!*—yet to the critics, especially in America, his "truthful" depiction of life was still of prime importance. O'Neill himself, like his acknowledged master, Johan August Strindberg, came to feel quite early in his career that the naturalistic mode constricted his imagination, and he began to experiment with other modes of dramatic expression. His critics, however, for the most part remained loyal to naturalism and hardly noticed his attempts to bring new forms to the American stage. It is, for instance, significant that the words "expressionism" or "expressionistic" do not appear in the reviews of *The Emperor Jones* by Heywood Broun, *The Hairy Ape* by Alexander Woollcott, *All God's Chillun Got Wings* by T. S. Eliot, and *The Great God Brown* by Gilbert Gabriel. To be sure, the reviewers are aware of certain elements of technique that seem novel—such as the use of masks or of special sound effects, the "fantastic" nature of plot, and the resort to distortion in setting and gesture—but emphasis is still laid upon "true talk" (Woollcott), "exact portrayal of a possible negro" (Eliot), and "splendidly positive language" (Gabriel).

CRITICAL RECEPTION IN EUROPE

In Europe the critics received O'Neill with equal enthusiasm but greater understanding. By 1946, when George Jean Nathan published his "Critical Summation" of O'Neill's impact on world criticism in the *American Mercury,* he found that in France, Italy, Russia, the Scandinavian countries, Rumania, Greece, Australia, and China the attitude had been "extremely favorable"; in Germany, highly appreciative; and only in England "lukewarm or chilly." We know that now, since the London production of *Long Day's Journey,* the critical attitude toward O'Neill in England too has become favorable, and many of his earlier plays are being revived. Perhaps one reason for England's resistance to these earlier plays can be found in the fact that nineteenth-century realism and naturalism—Robertson, Pinero, Jones, Galsworthy—dominated the English stage much longer than it did the stages of other European countries. Today, when Beckett, Ionesco, the later O'Casey, Pinter, and Mortimer are accepted, at least in off-West End, the experimental O'Neill too can be accepted. . . .

Many European critics hailed O'Neill as the voice of "America," the untired voice of a still young country, a sort of twentieth-century Walt Whitman shouting his dramatic yawp over the stages of the world. But there were a few critics, like Rudolf Kommer and Julius Bab, who perceived that O'Neill, while writing in terms of his age and his country, was actually expressing—himself. Certainly his dramatic tradition was not American; one could clearly detect in his plays the "traces" of Ibsen, Strindberg, Wedekind, Freud, and other Europeans. These more perceptive critics took little stock in O'Neill's sociological, economic, or political "message" or wisdom; what they applauded was, in the words of Julius Bab, "the tireless curiosity with which O'Neill explored all theatric and dramatic forms." Kommer, especially, praised O'Neill for *not* being the voice of America but for possessing a voice of his own, for *not* representing "any group, movement . . . current or tendency"; O'Neill, he insisted, was "a personality, human and creative, sincere and isolated."

CHAPTER 2

Themes and Issues in O'Neill's Plays

READINGS ON
EUGENE O'NEILL

An Overview of O'Neill's Plays

Margaret Loftus Ranald

Margaret Loftus Ranald assesses Eugene O'Neill's achievement in terms of his intellectual range and his desire to challenge traditional theatrical forms and techniques. O'Neill was a relentless experimenter, says Ranald, who continually pushed commonly accepted notions of drama, made innovative use of mythology, masks, and interior monologues, and provoked his audiences with challenging subjects such as race relations, abortion, adultery, and dysfunctional family relationships.

Ranald concludes that O'Neill was preeminently successful in presenting his vision of the human condition. In over sixty plays O'Neill, with high seriousness and sardonic humor, explores humanity's powerlessness before fate, the depersonalization of individuals in a modern, materialistic society, and the tenuousness of human relationships.

Margaret Loftus Ranald is a professor of English at Queen's College, City University of New York. In addition to numerous articles concerning O'Neill, Shakespeare, and theater history, she is the author of *The Eugene O'Neill Companion* and *Shakespeare and His Social Context: Essays in Osmotic Knowledge and Literary Interpretation.* Ranald is also an associate editor of *International Bibliography of Theater.*

The author of over 60 completed and partly written plays, Eugene O'Neill brought high seriousness to the American drama. From the beginning of his career, he reacted against the escapist theatre of his actor-father, epitomized by James O'Neill Sr.'s financially successful role as Edmond Dantès in *The Count of Monte Cristo.*

From the earliest plays (produced at the Provincetown Playhouse, Massachusetts, and its New York City theatre) O'Neill presented the perennial cosmic theme, humanity's powerlessness before fate. This is shown in enslavement to the sea in the S.S. Glencairn plays, *Ile* and *Anna Christie*. But equally as important, O'Neill continually insisted on the need of an artist to honor and use his gift. Throughout the O'Neill canon, denial of one's talent causes destruction of the individual, from Robert Mayo in *Beyond the Horizon*, O'Neill's first Broadway success, to Simon Harford in *A Touch of the Poet*. This theme is also the basis of other plays in that proposed saga of American acquisitiveness, "A Tale of Possessors, Self-Dispossessed".

Another important O'Neill theme is that of "belonging", and this shades into nostalgia for a pre-mechanistic past— the days of sail, for instance. He excoriates the depersonalization of the individual in modern society, particularly in the expressionistic drama *The Hairy Ape*, in which Yank, the servant and apostle of the machine, is psychologically castrated by a female member of the ruling class in a mere seven words: "Take me away! Oh! The filthy beast!". This play is the only one in which the politics of class struggle are fully relevant, though two other works, *The Personal Equation* and *The Reckoning* (published 1988), are concerned with aspects of trade unionism.

RACE RELATIONS IN O'NEILL'S PLAYS

O'Neill was a pioneer in theatrical race relations. His very early one-act play *Thirst* had a West-Indian mulatto sailor, played by O'Neill himself, as one of the three characters on a life raft, while a second one-acter, *The Dreamy Kid*, concerned a small-time black gangster. This was the first occasion on which a white company hired an entire company of black actors to play black roles. *The Emperor Jones* went further by making use of integrated casting. Charles Gilpin, a black actor, created the central role in this Jungian-influenced expressionistic monologue portraying African-American history in reverse. Gilpin's success led to a partial opening of the doors to professional theatre for African-American actors.

Even more controversial was *All God's Chillun Got Wings*, recounting the marriage of the white girl, Ella Downey, to the African-American Jim Harris. Though this play caused a furor of prejudice on its original production, race relations are not its true theme, which, once again, is that of the artist-figure, here the ambitious law student, Jim Harris, who is thwarted and destroyed by his wife's possessiveness and lack of understanding.

O'NEILL'S USE OF MASKS

Ever the experimenter, O'Neill now turned to masks, and with *The Great God Brown* he offered his first fully masked play. He had already used an African mask in *All God's Chillun* as a means of showing the threat offered to the white, effete Ella Downey by Jim's alien and elemental world. In *The Hairy Ape* he had employed masks in the Fifth Avenue expressionistic scene, at the suggestion of Blanche Hays, the costume designer; but in *The Great God Brown* he wished to develop "a drama of souls" to gain "insight into the inner forces motivating the actions and reactions of men and women". As O'Neill himself put it, "one's outer life passes in a solitude haunted by the masks of others; one's inner life passes in a solitude haunted by the masks of oneself" (in his "Memoranda on Masks").

With *Lazarus Laughed*, a "play for an imaginative theatre", in four acts, eight scenes, and over 420 roles, O'Neill used masks for all characters except Lazarus, who celebrates life, having no fear of death. In this play, which goes beyond the economic limits of the professional theatre and has, at the time of writing, yet to achieve a fully professional performance, he tried to re-create ritual theatre, analogous to that which grew out of the ancient worship of Dionysus, which could serve again as "practical interpretation and celebration of life". Later, in *Days Without End*, he returned to the use of masks to distinguish the protagonist John from his antagonist *alter ego*, Loving.

O'NEILL'S EXPERIMENTATION WITH DRAMATIC FORM

O'Neill tested his theories of drama in the further experimental plays *The Fountain* and *Marco Millions*. With the sympathetic cooperation of Kenneth Macgowan as director, and Robert Edmond Jones as scene designer, he aimed at presenting total theatre, or plastic theatre, pressing on the limits of the stage, and applying imaginative techniques to dramatic form, theme, and scenic design. Ambitiously, he now wished to educate his audience in philosophy through a comprehensive theatrical experience. These plays, along with *Lazarus Laughed,* are all intellectually and speculatively important, but are only stageable in the theatre of the mind even though O'Neill showed in them some of his best writing and deepest poetic thought, in attempting a synthesis of history, satire, religion, reconciliation, and love.

His next technical experiment was the nine-act drama *Strange Interlude,* which dealt openly with the taboo subjects of abortion and adultery. Here, O'Neill later wished he had used masks, but instead employed interior monologue to convey the secret thoughts of the protagonists. Thus, the double action portrays outward reality contrasted with inward contemplation and evaluation of that reality. Conflicts, then, are both overt and psychic as O'Neill also played with time, projecting the final act 17 years beyond the date of the play's original production. The true theme is the psychological life of woman in the three manifestations imaged by O'Neill—mother, wife, mistress-whore—within a dramatic structure of gestation and the eternal return.

O'NEILL'S USE OF MYTHOLOGY

O'Neill's tragic vision, with its solid grounding in the resonances of myth, naturally led him to attempt the creation of a new, original mythology to reflect the concerns of the 20th century, a task that occupied him for the remainder of his life. Two plays, *Desire Under the Elms* and *Dynamo,* demonstrate O'Neill as an excellent *myth user,* but less successful as *myth maker.* Consequently, it is something of a tragedy for American drama that he spent so much of his productive life endeavoring to produce the ultimate myth of acquisitive American civilization in his proposed 11-play cycle "A Tale of Possessors, Self-Dispossessed".

In *Mourning Becomes Electra,* his next experiment in mythology, O'Neill re-created the classical trilogy format in its three full-length plays, *The Homecoming, The Hunted,* and *The Haunted.* Here, as with his larger experiments in total theatre, *The Fountain* and *Lazarus Laughed,* O'Neill appealed to the theatre of the mind, rather than the limitations of the professional stage. In this work, his most creative employment and amalgamation of diverse myths he used the fate of the House of Atreus as a basis, deliberately adapting the myth to an archetypal American time and place fashioning "a modern drama in which the Greek fates are replaced by forces which are more comprehensible in an age without religion and without commitment to gods". O'Neill then turned to myth-making. After the completion of *Marco Millions* he began to think in terms of a trilogy to be called "Myth-Plays for the God-Forsaken". Here he hoped to reforge a modern belief independent of established religions and suitable for a world that had lost its spiritual way. He set out to reveal the sickness of materialistic American society as he attacked "repressive organized religion with its fear of human sexuality and physicality". In the first of these plays, *Dynamo*, O'Neill seized on the suggestion of Henry Adams in "The Dynamo and the Virgin" that for the 20th century the force and energy of the dynamo are analogous to the medieval cultural and constructive creativity generated by worship of the Virgin. O'Neill portrayed the fate of young Reuben Light who worships the dynamo as his anthropomorphic earth mother/goddess and is destroyed by it, perhaps because he is unworthy. After the unsuccessful *Days Without End*, the second play of this abortive trilogy, O'Neill abandoned the project.

However, *Days Without End* represents a development that led to the last cycle, "A Tale of Possessors, Self-Dispossessed", which "planned to use the saga of one family to illustrate the central theme of the corrupting influence of possessions upon their owners"; and more than coincidentally, it emphasizes a series of marriages and family dramas in much the same way as O'Neill finally used his own family to create a new mythology of human relationships.

O'NEILL'S PORTRAYAL OF FAMILY

Familial relationships are, in fact, a central thematic strand of much of O'Neill's work, from *Bread and Butter* and *Servitude;* in the latter a major theme is "Servitude in love! Love in servitude!". This is taken up in *Welded, The First Man*, by Elsa Loving in *Days Without End*, and by both Nora and Sara Melody in *A Touch of the Poet*, though later, in *More Stately Mansions*, Sara displays the acquisitive, sensual side of her personality. But O'Neill's family members are almost invariably at each other's throats—except in *Ah, Wilderness!*, a traditionally sentimental, comedic exercise in wish-fulfilled remembrance.

Even *The Iceman Cometh* is a kind of familial drama, because the denizens of the "Last Chance Bar" form a community which is temporarily shattered by the intrusion of Theodore Hickman, who brings death and disruption to those who are bonded by their withdrawal from life. Conversely, *Hughie,* a self-contained monologue, features, in "Erie" Smith, a character who is trying to reach out, "to belong", one who, like the characters of *The Iceman Cometh* and Cornelius Melody in *A Touch of the Poet,* takes refuge in the Ibsenesque "saving lie" to continue living. In effect, all "these last plays continue the theme of the mask which hides the psychic identity of the individual . . . while the action shows characters being stripped of pretense". . . .

With his Pulitzer Prize–winning *Long Day's Journey into Night* and *A Moon for the Misbegotten,* O'Neill developed his personal, psychological myth-making into high art, paradoxically by returning to realistic techniques. With selective memory, he whitewashed himself by omitting his first marriage, and made peace with his father and brother, paying tribute to their idiosyncrasies, while sympathizing with their weaknesses. However, he never forgave his mother. She remains unhistorically unsolvable, just as the portrait of James O'Neill as irremediable alcoholic and miser is untrue. Indeed, O'Neill seems never to have appreciated the struggle Ella O'Neill underwent in overcoming her addiction to morphine. But then again, his attitude towards women throughout the plays is flawed. For him, woman is virgin/mother/whore, one who must serve man: Josie Hogan in *A Moon for the Misbegotten* is her earth-mother epitome as she cradles Jamie's head in her lap in a Pietà.

Ironically, by the end of his working life, O'Neill had become disenchanted with the theatre—*Hughie* was the only completed play of another projected series, entitled "By Way of Obit". Each of the proposed eight monologue-plays was meant to consist of one scene, with one character and one life-size marionette, the Good Listener. The reactions of this listener, if one can take *Hughie* as representative, are almost entirely non-verbal, and clues to his reactions are in the stage directions, rather than in the dialogue.

"Eclectic to a fault" (as one critic, Christopher Bigsby, has described O'Neill) and permanently experimental, O'Neill's distinguishing characteristics include high seriousness, contrived mass effects, heavy use of irony, melodramatic situations, sardonic humour, imaginative intellectual exploration, and genuine dramatic talent. In his synthesis of myth, past and present, he was pre-eminently successful in giving to the American theatre a unique sense of the tragic human condition.

Themes in O'Neill's Plays

Anthony S. Abbott

Anthony S. Abbott refers to O'Neill as a frustrated idealist, a dreamer. The conflict between ideals and the reality of life's harsh experiences generates the playwright's central subject matter in his early plays. Throughout his dramas, O'Neill focuses on humanity's natural impulses to seek the ideal, to discover and nourish a genuine sense of self, and to break through the masks of material life to unite with a spiritual force. Ultimately, however, O'Neill believes that these impulses will be thwarted by reality.

Abbott maintains that this illusion/reality conflict is exemplified in *The Iceman Cometh.* Here the main characters, cloaked in dreams, are one by one stripped by reality. At the end, the characters must face the one final reality, death.

Anthony S. Abbott is professor of English at Davidson College in North Carolina. He is the author of *Shaw and Christianity.* He has also written books in the Barron's Book Notes series.

Perhaps the place to begin is with Edmund's library in *Long Day's Journey into Night.* Much of the great scene in the fourth act between father and son is a kind of literary conflict, with Edmund throwing his authors against his father's—Balzac and Whitman, Strindberg and Shaw and Ibsen, Baudelaire and Dowson, against Shakespeare, Dickens, and the Bible. James and Edmund are like debaters, quoting their favorite passages as evidence to support their positions. Edmund's books, of course, are pretty much the ones Eugene O'Neill himself read at that time or would read and reread during his period of confinement at the Gaylord Farm Sanatorium in 1912 and 1913. O'Neill was twenty-four in 1912, and his ideas had been strongly shaped both by his reading and by the turbulent experiences of his adolescence and early manhood. By the time he began to write one-act plays in 1913, he had been married and divorced, he had fathered a son, he had spent two years at sea, and he had almost committed suicide while living at Jimmy the Priest's, a waterfront dive in lower Manhattan that would become the setting for two of his most famous plays, *Anna Christie* and *The Iceman Cometh.*

This tension between literature and life, between those books that embody the playwright's vision and ideals and those life experiences that continually thwart the fulfillment of those ideals, forms the central subject matter of O'Neill's plays; and though both the dramatic form in which the playwright expresses the tension evolves and the attitude toward the subject changes with the evolution of form, the subject is there from the beginning, and it never ceases to obsess the playwright. In some ways O'Neill belongs more with Ibsen and Shaw and Strindberg, his heroes, than with Pirandello and Brecht, his contemporaries. He is, like the earlier playwrights, a frustrated idealist, a dreamer, almost one of the Hegelians. But finally, his dream of a breakthrough fails him; and in the late plays he joins Pirandello in asking for human compassion rather than some encompassing vision of truth.

In his perceptive essay "O'Neill's Search for a 'Language of the Theatre,'" Robert F. Whitman describes the central tension of O'Neill's plays in this way: "Characteristically, the impulse toward the ideal, frustrated by life, brings cynicism and despair; the impulse toward faith, frustrated by life, leads to skepticism; the impulse to love, frustrated by life, leads to hate or smothering possessiveness; the impulse to create, frustrated by life, becomes destructive."

THE QUEST THEME

The quest theme is obvious. The natural impulses of human beings are toward the ideal; toward faith, love, creation; toward a higher order of being. But life frustrates our dreams and aspirations. Thus O'Neill's theme, as Whitman sees it, is "the eternal conflict between Man's aspirations and some intransigent, ineluctable quality in life which circumscribes and limits him, and frustrates the realization of those dreams which seem to make life worth living."

The quest motif is evident from the time of O'Neill's first

full-length play, *Beyond the Horizon,* which opened at the Morosco Theatre in February of 1920 and won O'Neill his first Pulitzer Prize. Robert Mayo is O'Neill's archetypal hero in embryo. He is a dreamer who longs for the sea, trapped on the farm. He reads books. Throughout O'Neill's work, books and the sea will stand as symbols of the search for a higher, deeper, fuller life. Robert sees that fuller life "beyond the horizon," and he has made up his mind to go in search of it, when "reality" intervenes in the form of Ruth. Ruth loves him, not his brother, Andy, whom he has supposed she loves, but she will not encourage him in his search, nor will she go with him. She is rooted in the farm. The joining of the two farms, so critical in the value system of the father, becomes possible with the marriage of Robert and Ruth, but it will also bring about Robert's destruction. Andy replaces Robert as the voyager, but the sea is not a natural life for him. He is not an explorer, a thinker, and he writes back prosaic postcards from ports of call, describing only the dirt in places Robert would have gloried in seeing. . . .

THE BELONGING THEME

The theme of "belonging" is picked up in the following year (1921) as the central issue of *The Hairy Ape.* Yank is another O'Neill dreamer, but a primitive and inarticulate one, a stoker on a transatlantic liner who has been shocked into awareness of himself by Mildred Douglas's terrified reaction to him when she visits the stokehole in the third scene. During the remainder of the play his characteristic pose is that of Rodin's[1] *The Thinker.* He is trying to figure out something, but he can't. *The Hairy Ape,* whether consciously or not, bears the stamp of D.H. Lawrence.[2] Yank is the passionate, elemental force in man. It is at peace with itself, comfortable in its primitive, animal joy. Mildred, her aunt, her father, and the characters who parade by on Fifth Avenue have lost that part of themselves. They have destroyed it, refined it to the point of nonexistence. They do not recognize Yank. Our human dilemma, as symbolized by Yank's, is how to move upward on the evolutionary scale, how to grow, without destroying the joyous or animal part of the self. This is a theme to which O'Neill will return again and again, especially in *Strange Interlude* and *Mourning Becomes Electra.*

1. French sculptor Auguste 2. English novelist

It is a mistake to accept Yank as simply the "hairy ape" of the title. When asked about the play's theme by George Jean Nathan, O'Neill responded, "I must dig at the roots of the sickness of today as I feel it—the death of the old God and the failure of science and materialism to give any satisfactory new one for the surviving primitive religious instinct to find a meaning for life in, and to comfort its fears of death with." Yank's desire to belong is a part of that "primitive religious instinct." Having lost his place in the world of the stokehole, he is groping hopelessly for meaning, for dignity, as Arthur Miller would call it, in a world that has nothing to offer him. As he stands before the gorilla cage, he reflects, "I ain't got no past to tink in, nor nothin' dats comin' on'y what's now—and dat don't belong." In O'Neill's world belonging means finding a place where a genuine self can be nourished and prosper. And that is all but impossible.

The third of O'Neill's important early plays, *The Emperor Jones* (1920), treats the theme somewhat differently. Less sympathetic than either Robert Mayo or Yank, Jones is farther back on the evolutionary scale. Robert and Yank have rejected the values of society and stand, however tentatively, at least on the edge of a breakthrough. Jones still believes in the material values of money and power, and the play is the story of his gradual movement toward self-understanding through what Doris Falk calls "the striking off of the masks of the self, layer by layer, just as bit by bit his emperor's uniform is ripped from his back." Jones's basic illusion is that he has no illusions; and even at the end of his ordeal he continues to believe in the superstition of the silver bullet. Perhaps he dies more at the beginning of his quest than as a result of it.

THE REALITY-ILLUSION THEME

In *Desire Under the Elms* (1924), the culminating play of the first period of O'Neill's career, we see the emergence of the reality-illusion theme in the form that will dominate for the next seven or eight years. The central figures, Abbie Putnam and Eben Cabot, are stronger figures than their predecessors in *Beyond the Horizon.* They are driven by darker and more complex passions, and their tragedy runs deeper than that of Robert Mayo, who is more a victim than a tragic hero. O'Neill's view of tragedy is closely related to the quest theme. In a frequently reprinted statement, O'Neill said to Arthur Hobson Quinn, "I'm always acutely conscious of the Force behind (Fate, God, our biological past creating our present, whatever one calls it—Mystery certainly) and of *the one eternal tragedy of Man in his glorious, self-destructive struggle to make the Force express him* instead of being, as an animal is, an infinitesimal incident in its expression" [italics mine].

For O'Neill the center of *Desire Under the Elms* is Abbie and Eben's "glorious, self-destructive struggle" to overcome both the materialism of ownership and the repressive Puritanism symbolized by Ephraim. At the beginning of the play Abbie is motivated primarily by greed, the desire to own something. Her first line is "It's purty—purty! I can't b'lieve it's really mine." "Yewr'n?" asks Cabot. "Mine!" The desire to own the farm underlies the tragedy of the play. The sheriff, blind to the tragic implications of ownership, ends the play with the ironic line, "It's a jim-dandy farm, no denyin'. Wished I owned it." The painful process of moving from desire for things and sexual desire to love for one another ennobles Abbie and Eben. They attempt to make the force express them through that love, but the only way Abbie knows how to prove her love to Eben is to kill the child, and so the ending becomes both glorious and self-destructive.

We see the same kind of victory in defeat in O'Neill's most ambitious play, *Mourning Becomes Electra* (1931). Here again, as so often in O'Neill, reality finally defeats human attempts to gain freedom and happiness, but the victory of reality is less oppressive than in many of the other plays, because Lavinia, the Electra figure, freely chooses to close herself in the house in order to expiate the Mannon curse. Mourning does become Electra. The play is built around the familiar contrast between life and death. In Part I, *Homecoming*, death is represented primarily by Ezra Mannon and the Mannon house. We also sense death in the Puritan austerity of Lavinia, who is in every respect her father's daughter. Christine Mannon and Adam Brant try to break out of the repressive world of the Mannons through the life-giving freedom of sexuality. Sex in the Mannon household is associated with sin, and the only way that Christine and Adam can find to overcome this repressive attitude is to kill Ezra. But murder only begets murder, and all of the characters' attempts to gain freedom and peace, to find "the blessed isles," end in disaster.

In Part II, *The Hunted*, the life figures, Christine and Adam, are destroyed by Orin and Lavinia, the death figures, the life deniers; but the murder of Adam and Christine's suicide serve only to unhinge Orin and force Lavinia to realize that she can never live in the ordinary world. For a moment in the final play, *The Haunted,* it seems as if life will be victorious. Vinnie, changed by her trip to the South Seas, has cast off the death-in-life of the Mannon house, and we see her for the first time as a woman. Away from the sexually inhibiting world of New England, she has found sexual fulfillment. She has become her mother rather than her father. But O'Neill's tragic view is uncompromising. Orin's suicide shows her that marriage to Peter will only extend the Mannon curse, and she makes the life-denying decision to end the curse by locking herself in the house in order to save others from suffering. Her defeat is a defeat for life, but she has succeeded, to go back to O'Neill's words, in making the Force express her, "instead of being, as an animal is, an infinitesimal incident in its expression." There is dignity and nobility in her final renunciation; if the play depicts the final triumph of reality over dream, it also depicts in Vinnie a human being who is strong enough to live without illusions. . . .

THE DESIRE FOR SPIRITUALITY

"Man is born broken. He lives by mending. The grace of God is glue!" says Billy in the fourth act of *The Great God Brown.* "The mistake began when God was created in a male image," says Nina. The statements are closely related. There is a strong religious element in the plays written between 1925 and 1934, an element that shows O'Neill struggling with a symbolism adequate to express the spiritual statement the playwright is trying to make. Whether in the plays we have looked at or in the less successful experiments like *Dynamo* and *Days Without End,* there is always that thematic thrust toward reunion with the feminine figure, the mother God.

O'Neill combines his own obsessive Freudianism with a kind of latent feminist theology by attacking the identification of religion with the hard, masculine tradition of American Puritanism. His heroes struggle desperately to break through the "strange interlude" of this life, break through the meaningless electrical displays of the male God, "whose chest thunders with egotism," into a reunion with the natural, life-affirming force of the feminine. In a Jungian sense, O'Neill's male heroes are searching for a completion of the self, which the hard father God, whether it calls itself Mayo, Cabot, or Leeds, consistently denies. During this period O'Neill demonstrates most forcefully his affinity with Strindberg,[3] especially the Strindberg of *A Dream Play*, the tortured and disillusioned idealist trying to fight through the masks of the material world to union with the spiritual or feminine element, symbolized in *A Dream Play* by the Daughter of Indra. . . .

THEMATIC STRUCTURE IN *THE ICEMAN COMETH*

The Iceman Cometh (1946) is the archetype for all the plays. It takes place in Harry Hope's saloon (in reality Jimmy the Priest's, where O'Neill stayed frequently between 1909 and 1912), in the year 1912, a critical year in the playwright's life and the same year in which *Long Day's Journey* is set. The characters may be divided into two groups: (1) Harry Hope and the workers and roomers, and (2) Larry Slade, Don Parrit, and Hickey. The members of the first group are all sustained by illusions about both their past and their future. The characters in the first group parallel, in ways, the members of the Ekdal family in Ibsen's *The Wild Duck*, and Hickey is clearly derived in certain of his traits from Gregers Werle. In O'Neill's play the term *vital lie* has been replaced by *pipe dream*. Whether they are the same and whether O'Neill's attitude toward illusion is different from Ibsen's we can only surmise after some analysis.

Harry, an old ward politician, has not left the rooming house since his wife died, and he dreams of the day when he will take a walk around the block and renew his political career. His brother-in-law, Ed Mosher, plans to get a job with the circus. Pat McGloin hopes to clear his name and have himself restored to duty with the police force, and Willie Oban, remembering his potential in law school, thinks of getting a job in the district attorney's office after his brilliant defense of Pat gets the policeman reinstated. Joe Mott, the Negro, dreams of running a black gambling house, while Piet Wetjoen, the Boer "General," and Cecil Lewis, the English "Captain," relive the Boer War and dream each of returning to his native land. James Cameron, "Jimmy Tomorrow," thinks of the day when he will return triumphantly to the

3. Swedish playwright August

newspaper, and the last of the group, Hugo Kalmar, periodi-
cally awakens from his drunken stupor to dream of the
future triumph of the "Movement" (IWW, or International
Workers of the World). The help at the rooming house and
bar parallels the clientele. Rocky Pioggi, the night bartender,
thinks of himself as a "business manager," when he is really
a pimp for Pearl and Margie, two prostitutes who comfort
each other by thinking of themselves as tarts. Chuck, the day
bartender, plans to marry another prostitute, Cora, and they
dream of a farm in the country far from the corruption of
Harry's bar.

Into this world of pipe dreams steps Theodore Hickman
(Hickey), who, like Gregers Werle, is determined to make
each of them start life anew on the foundation of truth. No
longer will they need the escape of alcohol or foolish pipe
dreams. Each of them must make his dream a reality, each
must do the thing he has been talking about. The result is
near-disaster. One by one, the characters are stripped naked,
and deprived of drink and dreams, they become nervous,
ugly, depressed. Conflicts that had been playful become real.
Tempers flare, and racial prejudice erupts. One by one, the
roomers leave the bar to go into the "real" world, and by
night they have all returned—sullen, remorseful, defeated
by life. It is only just before the very end of the play, when
Hickey admits that he was crazy and, in a sense, gives them
their vital lies back, that they regain their peace, their sense
of humor, their fellowship. Like the members of the Ekdal
family, they are best left with their pipe dreams. Dr. Relling
has been vindicated.

But, as both Eric Bentley and C.W.E. Bigsby have demon-
strated, the reality-illusion conflict is not the play's central
theme. *The Iceman Cometh* may be more O'Neill's version of
It Is So than his version of *The Wild Duck*. The play's three
central figures—Hickey, Parrit, and Slade—are best understood when approached from a different perspective, that of
the love-hate conflict. Hickey, while he pretends that he no
longer needs illusions, has really preserved the greatest illusion of all—the illusion that he loved his wife. Parrit, who
parallels Hickey throughout, continually confesses that he is
responsible for his mother's capture by the police, but like
Hickey, he never confesses his true motive until he acciden-
tally blurts it out near the end. Both Parrit and Hickey illustrate what can happen when love is replaced by hate. Torn

by guilt themselves, neither can leave the others alone. Neither can develop what Bigsby calls "a level of imaginative sympathy," which would allow them to develop real compassion for others. Hickey destroys the peace of Harry's roomers because he hasn't the courage to face himself, just as Gregers Werle turns his own self-hatred on the Ekdal household. Parrit cannot face himself either until the very end, when he commits, with Larry Slade's support, the act he really came to Harry Hope's for—his own suicide.

O'Neill, much more pessimistic than Ibsen, finally, does not leave us truth as an option. *The Wild Duck* implies that truth is better under the right conditions. *The Iceman Cometh* gives us only, in Edwin Engel's words, "dreams, drunkenness, and death." And neither dreams nor death are treated so romantically as in the earlier plays. Death is not a return to the earth mother or to the unity of things; death is the final reality—the end. This is the view embodied by Larry Slade. "I'm the only real convert to death Hickey made here," he says at the play's end, and he means it. His experience with Parrit and Hickey has destroyed the last of his illusions, and he will not return to his role as the grandstand "foolosopher" and friend of the outcast. At the play's end he stares grimly ahead, waiting for death to take him.

The Role of Women in O'Neill's Plays

Jane Torrey

Psychologist Jane Torrey assesses the O'Neill characters who struggle against racial prejudice and class oppression. O'Neill understood racial prejudice and depicts black Americans as oppressed individuals, not as stereotypes. He also poignantly portrays lower-class white men who struggle against unfair and overwhelming circumstances. Torrey argues, however, that O'Neill is not as sensitive in his portrayal of women. Unlike his male characters, the playwright's females accept oppression and exploitation as inherent to their sex, not circumstantial. Hence, his female characters, motivated only by their men's needs, do not struggle against their female role. In short, Torrey suggests that for O'Neill a woman's destiny is to serve a man, whereas a man's destiny is to seek personal fulfillment.

Jane Torrey teaches psychology at Connecticut College. She has published numerous articles and reviews in *Contemporary Psychology, Harvard Educational Review,* and *Reading Research.* She is also the author of "Phases of Feminist Re-Vision in the Psychology of Personality" in *Teaching of Psychology.*

As a teacher of psychology, I have explored literary ground in search of realistic portrayals of individual personalities to use as a basis for class discussions on personality theory. Characters in works of literature are better material for practice in applying psychology than are people described in psychological case reports. This may be because the information artistic writers provide consists of feelings and actions in concrete situations rather than abstract dimen-

Excerpted from "O'Neill's Psychology of Oppression in Men and Women" by Jane Torrey, in *Eugene O'Neill's Century: Centennial Views on America's Foremost Tragic Dramatist,* edited by Richard F. Moorton Jr. Copyright © 1991 by Richard F. Moorton Jr. Reproduced with permission of Greenwood Publishing Group, Inc., Westport, Conn.

sions or because their descriptions are uncontaminated with the theoretical biases of the reporting psychologist. However that may be, the psychology of personality is largely the creation of clinical practitioners dealing with neurotics, and therefore the most useful fictional "cases" for my purposes are tortured souls. That makes O'Neill's plays a treasure trove of useful materials.

O'NEILL'S CHARACTERS STRUGGLE AGAINST OPPRESSION

Among the troubled circumstances O'Neill wrote about were many kinds of social-group oppressions. He had many friends who were struggling against the disadvantages of class or race, and he possessed both the interest and the understanding to make them subjects of his work. His intimacy with people on the lower rungs of society made it possible for him not only to sympathize with them but also to see things from their point of view. He knew they had aspirations for their own identity, power, and transcendence like their more fortunate brothers. His men, no matter how degraded, took for granted their right to self-respect and self-determination. Like other men, they had need of women, and they expected their women to help them achieve their goals without necessarily feeling an obligation in return. There are men like this in the real world, and O'Neill's portraits of men, oppressed and otherwise, are apparently drawn from his experience.

O'Neill was exceptional among white Americans in that he understood racial as well as class oppression. He broke ground in the American theater by making clear that the problems of black Americans were caused by whites and by portraying blacks as real men, not unlike white men, rather than in terms of the traditional stereotypes. He even deviated from custom by insisting that black actors portray them instead of the traditional whites in black makeup. Brutus Jones in *The Emperor Jones* enjoys being the boss as much as any man. He doesn't seem to have much trouble with self-esteem, and his conscious motivation is to take care of himself. If he can't be emperor, he can at least be free and financially independent. Nobody else, male or female, figures in his life. Even his unconscious, which pursues and defeats him, doesn't tie him to any particular persons. It is a collective rather than a personal unconscious. In *All God's Chillun Got Wings*, Jim is a black man who dares to marry a white woman because he loves her. He moves to France and then home again to accommodate Ella. He also has ambition to get ahead in the world, but like many other O'Neill men, he has great need of a woman's support and confidence, and it is Ella's unwillingness to believe in him that defeats him. Ella's character shows O'Neill's rare insight into the unconscious and ambivalent racism so often found in white Americans. She loves a black man enough to marry him but is still unable to conquer the ingrained attitudes of her race.

In *The Dreamy Kid*, Abe "Dreamy" Saunders does stay with his dying mother even though the police are after him, but he does it more out of fear that leaving her will bring bad luck than out of any sense of obligation to her. He doesn't seem to care one way or the other about his devoted girl friend who wants to die with him.

O'Neill also understands class oppression well. All the "Icemen" belong to the underclass, but all have ambitions for self-actualization. Some of them have hang-ups about their women, but in no case is it unselfish devotion. Parritt feels guilty about having betrayed his mother, but he does feel she deserved it for not having met his needs. Larry is represented as having been ruined by the same woman, but the implication is that she was at fault for not having been devoted to him. Harry Hope's wife is blamed for his agoraphobia. She was always trying to make him go out. But nothing is said about any obligation he had to her. Hickey is perhaps the most egregious case. He blames Evelyn for his failings because she was *too* devoted to him and then uses her "fault" to justify his killing her in order to effect his own escape from guilt. All of these men seem to have needed their women but not to have considered that their women needed them.

Yank, the seagoing furnace stoker, is oppressed, exploited, and denigrated by society, but, like many women, he accepts his position and glories in it. The event that destroys his self-respect is the discovery that others regard him as disgusting subhuman life, and then, unlike O'Neill's women, he rebels and, furthermore, seeks by his rebellion to gain dignity and meaning for his own existence.

O'Neill's Oppressed Female Characters

Although men struggling with circumstance is one of O'Neill's more persistent themes, and social-group oppression is one of the oppressive circumstances, it is not so for women. He does not seem to see sex as a circumstance but rather as an inner nature. He portrayed many oppressed women, but his idea of an exploited woman's point of view was different. His women tended to be completely fulfilled by their relationship with men. They were not concerned with any individual achievements. It was their devotion and obligation to their men that dominated their motivation. It is as though they took oppression and exploitation for granted as the destiny of their sex. Thus his women do not struggle against their female role but act as though it were their very essence. Doris Nelson pointed out that in the case of women O'Neill almost never suggests that they have any motivations other than those involved in their relationships with men. There are many women in his plays who might have been but weren't motivated by anything other than their men's needs. For several of them class position suggests a possible career or other motivation for achievement. Nina of *Strange Interlude*, for example, was a professor's daughter and the woman in the lives of a businessman, a physician, and a successful writer. Yet she never discusses anything with any of them except her relationships with her men. She explicitly identifies herself through those connections when she says

> My three men! . . . I feel their desires converge in me! . . . to form one complete beautiful male desire which I absorb . . . and am whole . . . they dissolve in me, their life is my life . . . I am pregnant with the three! . . . husband! . . . lover! . . . father! . . . and the fourth man! . . . little man! . . . little Gordon! . . . he is mine too! . . . that makes it perfect!

Deborah and Sara of *More Stately Mansions* are both intelligent women, educated after the manner of women in their time; yet they are as identified with their man, their son and husband, respectively, as is Sara's relatively ignorant mother, Nora, of *A Touch of the Poet*. Lavinia is as capable as her brother Orin in *Mourning Becomes Electra*; yet all her motivations are derived from her relationships with the men in her life.

There are a few possible exceptions. Parritt's mother was devoted to her revolution, and Mary Tyrone still thinks wishfully of her lost career as a nun or a pianist. She yearns even more to be able to fulfill her chosen "career" as a proper lady of a proper family. In some of O'Neill's early work he shows an awareness of the power of conventional relationships between men and women to stifle the woman's potential and subordinate her to the man. Thus the title of the play *Servitude* refers to woman's oppression in marriage, an oppression against which the play protests, though it does not repudiate marriage as an institution. But most of O'Neill's women have nothing and are nothing except through men. Some of the apparent exceptions are in fact part of the very pattern of female dependence from which they seem to diverge. Thus Anna Christie, for example, successfully rejects the condemnation of her father, Chris, and her suitor, Mat, for her experience as a prostitute; yet the result is not autonomy for Anna but her integration into the life of her two men as a conventional daughter and wife. Likewise, Abbie Putnam in *Desire Under the Elms* seeks her own fortune, but she does so through marriage to one man and ultimately gives up everything because of her love for another. Eleanor Cape, the actress in *Welded*, has her own career, but her most successful roles come from the plays of her husband, John, upon whom she is therefore professionally dependent, and by the end of the play, in spite of the struggles of the two to maintain their individuality in a loving relationship, she has become subordinated to his needs for a wife and mother.

Some of O'Neill's women, furthermore, possess a nearly incredible devotion to their men. Nora, Josie, Evelyn, and the women of *The Dreamy Kid* give more than seems humanly possible. Probably, there are women in the real world who are that selfless without noticeable reciprocation, but none of the real women in O'Neill's life compared with them, though Carlotta Monterey came closer than he had a right to expect. He could not have derived this image of women from his experience in the real world or from his personal relationships. Nor could his fictional women have been based upon the traditional stereotype of the feminine. They are not weak or dependent or even particularly submissive. They are strong and their strength is needed by the men they worship and who are often very dependent on them.

I said that I made use of O'Neill's characters in psychology as though they were examples of real people whose motives and responses could be explained in terms of psychological theories. In this respect I am doing something that literary critics also often do. Another way I might have followed the literary scholars in understanding O'Neill's work would have been to treat it as though his dramas were "thematic apperceptions," that is, products of his imagination that give insight into his own personality. I have come to regard that approach as more useful in understanding his female characters. Perhaps he imprisoned his women in the needs of their men because his own need for women was so great. Trudy Drucker quoted him as saying, "The role a woman should play is that of sacrifice to her man." That may be why his imagination produces so many women who have no other desires than to do just that. It may also be why so many of his men felt threatened and controlled by the women they need so much.

Nora shows the epitome of this sacrificial role in *A Touch of the Poet* when she answers Sara's criticism of her devotion to her "poet": "It's little you know of love. . . . It's when, if all the fires of hell was between you, you'd walk in them gladly to be with him. . . . That's love, and I'm proud I've known the great sorrow and joy of it!" Nora gets little from her husband, but she doesn't seem to expect much. The emotional connection between them is almost entirely one-sided. Josie is another woman who bears the whole burden of her relationship with Jamie. She knows he won't do anything for her except need her, and that is all she wants. Evelyn adopted the same pattern with Hickey, and all she gets in return is resentment and murder. According to him, it is a way of returning the favor.

The Role of Female Characters

Another aspect of O'Neill's portrayals of women is his inability to separate the different ways in which they devote themselves to men. Mother, wife, or whore can be incorporated into one woman. Nora is a mother as much as a wife to Melody. Their daughter Sara becomes a kind of whore in order to secure her mate and much later plays the whore at his request when he gets tired of her as a wife. At the same time he has trouble distinguishing her from his mother: "Sometimes I become so intensely conscious of your unity that you appear as one woman to me. I can't distinguish my wife from . . . [my mother]." Josie consciously impersonates a whoring woman while she offers herself as mother to Jamie in response to his needs. Sara tells Simon in the final line of *More Stately Mansions*, "Yes, I'll be your Mother, too, now, and your peace and happiness and all you'll ever need in life!"

Although O'Neill expects women to be mothers as well as lovers and wives, it is only important that they be mothers to the man, not necessarily to his children. The husband-father role would involve *him* in some obligation to her and the children. O'Neill's women are supposed to be devoted to men, but the men have no reciprocal obligations. It is the women, not the men, who are supposed to be pillars of strength for someone else. Sara's children are sent away to their grandmother or to school. "Ah, the children!" she said to Simon in *More Stately Mansions.* "Not that I don't love them with all my heart. But they're not my lover and husband! You come first!" Abbie of *Desire Under the Elms* carries this priority to the extreme by actually murdering the baby in the hope of holding on to its father. Robert Mayo in *Beyond the Horizon* seems to reverse the pattern of the female sacrificing herself for her man, since he gives up his dream of going to sea to stay on the farm and be a husband to Ruth and a father to their child, but the apparent inversion of the pattern only confirms the pattern it inverts. Because he is a man, Robert's dream is alien to the domesticity for which he sacrifices it. Therefore his sacrifice of his destiny for a woman is unnatural, and it blights his marriage and his life, since as a result the farm fails, Robert and his daughter die, and Ruth's life is ruined. The lesson could hardly be more clear: It is a man's destiny to realize his nature, not to live in service to a woman, and the penalty for defying this "law of nature" is disaster. In O'Neill's moral universe, a woman's destiny is to serve a man, whereas a man's destiny is to fulfill himself.

I have attempted to account for the contrast between the realistic and sympathetic portrayal of a wide variety of men in O'Neill's plays and the narrow selection of unrealistically devoted female personalities in his work by showing that his women, unlike his men, are drawn from his need, not from his experience. They are all variations on the mythic mother-wife-whore that haunted O'Neill's own life and that of his brother.

Self-Deception as a Theme in O'Neill's Late Plays

Laurin Porter

According to Laurin Porter, the American desire to reinvent oneself and start life afresh is a recurring theme in O'Neill's late plays. Porter indicates that O'Neill's major characters are often disgruntled with their present lives, and, as an escape or effort to bolster their pride, they attempt to construct a definition of themselves built on an earlier event or memory. But the reinvented life is fiction, not reality, and the characters generally pay a huge price for their self-deception.

Porter draws on two plays, *A Touch of the Poet* and *Poet, More Stately Mansions,* to illustrate this theme. In *A Touch of the Poet* the protagonist, Con Melody, loses his fortune and, to compensate for his economic blunders, creates an image for himself based on an event from his young adulthood when the prospects for the future looked promising. In *Poet, More Stately Mansions,* the protagonist Simon Harford creates a persona of a poet and writer, his youthful dream, but in reality becomes a hardened and cutthroat business mogul. Porter contends that neither protagonist can sustain the fiction of his reinvented life, and both disintegrate into greater pain and diminishment.

Laurin Porter teaches drama and modern literature at the University of Texas, Dallas. She is the author of *Possessors Dispossessed: The Late Plays of Eugene O'Neill.*

In chapter 6 of *The Great Gatsby,* two-thirds of the way through the novel, Nick Carroway finally learns the truth about Gatsby's past. The flashy millionaire from West Egg, Long Island, it turns out, actually began his life as James Gatz, the son of a poor North Dakota couple:

Abridged from chapter one of *The Banished Prince: Time, Memory, and Ritual in the Late Plays of Eugene O'Neill* by Laurin Porter (Ann Arbor: UMI Research Press, 1988). Copyright ©1988 by Laurin R. Porter. Reprinted by permission of the author.

67

His parents were shiftless and unsuccessful farm people—his imagination had never really accepted them as his parents at all. The truth was that Jay Gatsby . . . sprang from his Platonic conception of himself. He was a son of God—a phrase which, if it means anything, means just that—and he must be about His Father's business, the service of a vast, vulgar, meretricious beauty. So he invented just the sort of Jay Gatsby that a seventeen-year-old boy would be likely to invent, and to this conception he was faithful to the end.

Fitzgerald's novel, which paints with brilliant strokes the portrait of the Jazz Age, also touches upon an ineffable longing of the culture at large. As Americans, we feel we should, at any point, be able to begin life over again, to reinvent ourselves. It is an impulse that goes as far back as the Puritans of Plymouth Plantation, who felt that their mandate was to reestablish God's kingdom on earth, to cut themselves off from the corruption of the Old World and start afresh on the green breast of the New. The names by which this enterprise was called—the New Canaan, the New Jerusalem, the City on the Hill—reverberate with religious intensity precisely because the Pilgrims saw it as the last chance God would offer to mankind. Theirs was a divine mission.

By the eighteenth century, although the fervor of the original settlers had shifted from theology to patriotism, the desire to redefine oneself was still evident in the individual as well as the culture at large. It informed Ben Franklin's list of virtues in the *Autobiography,* for example, as he optimistically set out to perfect himself (a list that is mirrored in the "General Resolves" of young Jimmy Gatz, written on the flyleaf of a *Hopalong Cassidy* book), just as it shaped the promise held forth by the frontier as a place to start life over.

The catch, of course, is the unavoidable reality of the past, which precludes the possibility of sailing off unencumbered into the future. Hester Prynne, protagonist of Hawthorne's *The Scarlet Letter,* learns that she cannot escape her past by discarding the scarlet letter; she must resume her burden again because it is part of her identity. She is the sum total of what she has been, and though the specific terms of her identity unfold variously as time passes, the pressure of her history continues to bear upon her present and, to a great extent, determine her future. Nor is spatial remove a solution, whether for Hester or for Huck Finn, whose decision to "light out for the territory" will be qualified by what he has already seen of "sivilization." We Americans, in our literature as in our lives, are a people obsessed with the future, following the grail of the American dream as "we beat on, boats against the current, borne back ceaselessly into the past."

O'NEILL'S LATE PLAYS

This present-past nexus is an issue that arises with notable frequency in the late plays of Eugene O'Neill, the son of an Irish Catholic immigrant, who inherits a cultural and intellectual legacy which can be traced back to the Puritans. It is almost entirely on these two traditions, the Irish Catholic and the Yankee, that he draws to create the works of his mature period, from roughly 1935 to 1943. During these years, O'Neill was at work on two projects of extremely ambitious scope: one, a cycle of historical plays, the other, a history of a much more personal nature, both dealing with the relationship of past to present. In 1935, having completed *Days Without End* and frustrated by a play called "The Career of Bessie Bowen" which would not come right, he began to work in earnest on a series of four plays, set in the latter half of the nineteenth century, about the offspring of characters he named Sara Melody and Simon Harford. Sara was to come from Irish immigrant stock; Simon would derive from a wealthy Yankee family. This merger would produce four sons whose careers in sailing, banking, the railroads, and politics would reflect some of the primary social, economic, and historical developments of the era. It was a project that grew like Topsy; it would not stay within the boundaries of an already ambitious undertaking. As the characters came to life and O'Neill began to trace their line in previous as well as future generations, the cycle expanded to first five, then seven, nine, and eventually eleven plays in all. The final plan was to encompass American history from 1755 to what was then essentially the present, 1932, by tracking the Melody-Harford family history through six generations.

O'Neill worked steadily on these plays up through the final years of the Depression, graphing the characters and their relationships on a huge chart; often he would have several plays going at once. Then in 1939 he put the cycle plays aside and began work on the second project, which was to become a cycle of a different sort. On June 8 of that year he began writing *The Iceman Cometh*, completing it by fall. Within the next four years, he completed *Long Day's Journey into Night*, *Hughie* (part of an intended cycle of one-acts entitled *By Way of Obit*), and *A Moon for the Misbegotten*. These plays draw, often with undisguised directness, upon people and experiences from O'Neill's past—his family, friends from his down-and-out Hell Hole days on the West Side of New York, experiences from his youth and young manhood.

Both sets of plays, the historical and the autobiographical cycles (for the second becomes a cycle in fact, if not in intention), manifest the concern with time noted earlier in American literature at large. Although the ways in which this theme is fleshed out vary from play to play, the interaction of past, present, and future remains a constant concern in both the autobiographical dramas (*Iceman, Hughie, Long Day's Journey,* and *A Moon for the Misbegotten*) and the historical plays (*A Touch of the Poet, More Stately Mansions,* and *The Calms of Capricorn*).

TIME THEME IN *A TOUCH OF THE POET*

For instance, in *A Touch of the Poet* (the only play of the historical cycle that O'Neill finished to his own satisfaction) the protagonist, Con Melody, is a first-generation Irish immigrant living in New England who has fallen on hard times. He has invested the fortune he brought with him from Ireland in a country inn, which the locals assure him will soon, by reason of its location on a projected thoroughfare, do a bustling business. But the highway never materializes, and Con is left presiding over a ramshackle, out-of-the-way inn, his fortune long gone and his dreams come to nought.

This is a severe tribulation for Con, who was born on an estate in the Old Country and still thinks of himself as an aristocrat. To maintain some shred of dignity, he reinvents himself—not, however, like Gatsby, out of whole cloth. He returns to a climactic moment in his past, when, as an officer in the British army, the Duke of Wellington had singled him out for praise on the battlefield at Talavera. Shortly thereafter he was promoted to major, and life seemed to open before him. He was handsome, fearless, and admired by his peers, and, although he had left a pregnant wife behind on his estate, he was an amorous suitor in the homes of the aristocracy of Spain and Portugal, where as a British officer he was afforded the respect denied him in his native Ireland. "Little did I dream then the disgrace that was to be my reward later on," Con says some nineteen years later.

To salvage his pride, Con insists on living the life of a gentleman. He refuses to work, hires a barkeeper he cannot afford, presses his wife and his daughter Sara into service as cook and waitress, and keeps a thoroughbred mare who is fed even if his family must go hungry. When the effort of maintaining this fiction begins to wear thin, he bolsters his pride with a fascinating act of will and imagination. Standing in front of a large mirror, he recites a verse from Byron's "Childe Harold," which insists that he is among the crowd, but not "of them," that he is superior to the riffraff around him. Con's self-creation also includes a yearly celebration of the pivotal Talavera experience, which takes place during the evening of *Poet*'s action.

Con's dilemma is at base one that stems from the inexorable workings of time. As the clock ticks on, he is removed ever further from that period in his life when dignity was available and dreams seemed within reach. To compensate for the subsequent diminishment he has experienced, he selects an epiphanic moment from his past and tries to bring its fullness to bear on the poverty of the present. But the past . . . does not let Con off so easily.

TIME THEME IN *POET, MORE STATELY MANSIONS*

Simon Harford, who marries Con's daughter Sara, is the protagonist of the sequel to *Poet, More Stately Mansions,* which O'Neill completed through the third draft. (It was revised and published posthumously in 1964 by Donald Gallup and Karl Ragnar Gierow of the Swedish Royal Dramatic Theatre.) Simon, too, tries to conquer time and make himself anew, though he adopts a different strategy from Con's (to whom he is linked by the "touch of the poet" that characterizes both). In the course of *Mansions,* Simon evolves through three different roles, trying on identities, as it were, to see which one fits. As a young man, rebelling against his wealthy father's businesslike approach to life, he retreats to a lake in the woods (an obvious parallel with [American writer Henry David] Thoreau), where he intends to write a book on the natural goodness of mankind and where, incidentally, he meets Sara. After they fall in love and get married, his Rousseauvian idealism lasts a bit longer, but as they have children and their financial needs become pressing, he becomes an entrepreneur and local businessman, much admired by his neighbors (the point at which *Mansions* takes up the story). He still pretends to work on his book in the evenings, but it is clear that he is only going through the motions. As the play progresses, Simon's successes get the better of him, and he hardens into a corporate mogul, even more ruthless and cutthroat than his father. At the same time he is torn between his wife, Sara, and his mother, Deborah, who represent different orientations toward time. When he marries Sara he cuts himself off from his past, choosing to build his future around his wife and sons. But as success possesses him and time carries him forward, he is attracted increasingly by the past and memories of childhood innocence, which he associates with moments spent with his mother in her garden retreat.

In both plays linear time—time of the clock and the calendar—generally brings diminishment and pain. Though superficially Con and Simon have opposite fates, Simon's success is as painful as Con's failure; as even a cursory examination of *Mansions* makes clear, the play traces Simon's increasingly apparent disintegration as he becomes less and less capable of reconciling wife and mother, business and family, self and world. Both characters, beset by present realities they can no longer tolerate, turn to memories of the past as an alternative. And both, as subsequent chapters will point out, ultimately revert to their origins. Con, by play's end, relinquishes his "Major Cornelius Melody" identity and takes on the role of Irish peasant; he "becomes" his father, old Ned Melody. Simon, after duplicating the success of a father he had earlier repudiated, reverts to an even earlier time so that, by the end of *More Stately Mansions,* after a confrontation with Deborah and Sara and a fall in which he injures his head, he returns to his childhood. The innocence he so intensely desires can only be achieved through loss of consciousness.

The theme of past and present is striking in both of these plays, as it is in all seven of the autobiographical-historical plays that culminate O'Neill's career. It brings to mind an oft-quoted line of Mary Tyrone's in *Long Day's Journey into Night*: "The past is the present, isn't it? It's the future too. We all try to lie out of that but life won't let us."

A Modern Playwright

John Gassner

John Gassner claims that Eugene O'Neill is America's first and perhaps greatest modern playwright. O'Neill's modernism is defined by his experimentation, his innovation, his individualism, and his "intense unease." During his career, O'Neill revolted against both the prevailing Puritan mores and middle-class complacency, machine worship, materialism, and opportunism. O'Neill moved the focus of American theater to the modern concerns of dramatizing subconscious pressures, psychology, and individualism.

Gassner also argues that O'Neill's modernism is expressed in his compulsion to depict humanity's failures tragically. A modern sense of alienation, despair, and damnation runs deeply through his plays. O'Neill's work often centers on a sense of loss—a loss of connection with God, nature, society, and family.

John Gassner is a lecturer on the dramatic arts, an independent producer on Broadway, and a member of the Pulitzer Prize drama jury. He is the editor of *Fifty Best Plays of the American Theatre, Eugene O'Neill,* and *Ideas in the Drama, Theatre at the Crossroads.*

Eugene O'Neill died at the age of sixty-five in Boston on November 27, 1953, but it is possible to maintain that he became the most alive playwright of the Fifties. More than any playwright of this decade, with the exception of Sean O'Casey, his work revealed those comprehensive interests and intensive explorations of human experience that distinguish a major dramatist. He was one of the very few playwrights of the midcentury stage who could arouse with some labor the same interest in life that about a dozen writers did with some ease

Excerpted by permission from *Theatre at the Crossroads* by John Gassner, Henry Holt and Company, publisher. For availability of other works by John Gassner, contact Applause Books, (212) 765-7880.

73

in modern fiction. It is not with a sense of loss but with a sense of lively recognition that we now associated O'Neill's name as play after play of his was revived or published and produced for the first time posthumously here and abroad.

It should be noted that one of the extremely rare twentieth-century dramatists of first rank was an American; this fact can only reinforce the widespread view that the contemporary American stage has been one of the most vigorous theatrical centers of the world. It is remarkable, too, that O'Neill won his reputation *twice* (once in the Twenties and once in the Fifties after his death), without coming up to the literary standards of the day or winning the approbation of literary critics.

O'NEILL'S REVIVAL IN THE 1950S

The return of O'Neill to the American stage in the Fifties and the renewed European interest in his work was a proper occasion for reëxamining his reputation. It had been examined about ten years before, when investigation was apparently concerned with demolishing O'Neill's fame. A new generation seemed to want to denigrate O'Neill, even if it had no new culture-hero to substitute. In the face of the onslaught his friends and admirers could only reflect that these young critics had few opportunities to see O'Neill's plays in adequate stage productions and that nothing charged against his work was really new.

With the Circle in the Square off-Broadway revival of *The Iceman Cometh* in 1956 and the impressive Broadway success of the long-deferred *Long Day's Journey into Night* during the same year O'Neill's return to favor and the discovery of his power by new audiences became apparent. In the season of 1956–57 he was represented on the New York stage alone by no less than four productions. Before 1960 two other O'Neill plays were on view in the New York theatre as well as abroad: *A Moon for the Misbegotten,* staged in the spring of 1957, and *A Touch of the Poet,* given a star-studded Broadway production in the 1958–59 season.

There can be no doubt that O'Neill represents virtually everything that is fundamentally modern about the American theatre. He reflects also all that has been modern about the European theatre in his restless experimentation, his avid cultivation of new ideas, his assertive individualism, and his intense unease. In many plays, he is most modern when his writing is most personal, and both his success and defeat parallel the course of our modernity. The success was that of a restless spirit honest enough to refuse to feel or think by rote, and the effect is often as provocative as a leading question and as exciting (if also as precarious) as a plunge down a waterfall. The defect of his talent may be summed up as a case of nearly continual straining for a negativeness or sense of desolation not always well founded and more conducive to darkness than to light, liberation, and final purgation.

O'Neill dignified the craft of playwriting in America. He made it a calling rather than a trade, and he gave playwrights, hitherto mostly hacks or entertainers but never oracles, a position of some importance in our cultural life. Winner of the Nobel Prize and author of plays staged in virtually all the capitals of Europe, he was our first dramatist of international standing. Though his power exceeded his skill on many an occasion, his craftsmanship was still sufficient to carry him through some of the most ambitious projects attempted in the Western theatre since Aeschylus wrote his trilogies twenty-four hundred years ago. O'Neill represented the avant-garde both in our country and in Europe in the Twenties, and his banner may still be seen fluttering in the vanguard. It is not too much to say that even our most venturesome living playwrights are generally discreet technicians in comparison with him. A leader of the experimental Little Theatre movement, led by his own play-producing organization, the Provincetown Players of Greenwich Village, and after 1920 the leading playwright also of the progressive wing of Broadway professionalism, O'Neill sparked a revolt of great moment against commonplace realism.

REVOLT AGAINST ACCEPTED MORES

O'Neill also expressed a general reaction against Victorian mores, especially against the Puritanism and Protestant ethic associated with American Victorianism. . . . Combined with a deeply felt (if also fashionably Bohemian) rejection of middle-class complacencies, machine-worship, dollar-idolatry, and the entire cult of go-getting opportunism, O'Neill's lofty individualism placed him in the forefront of those who began to modernize the content of American drama no less than its form. Both dramatic form and content were further modernized by his response to the spread of Freudianism or depth psychology that led to his attempting to dramatize subconscious pressures. The means he adopted for this purpose alone carried him into areas of experimentation which only venturesome playwrights dared enter and where only exceptionally adept ones could survive.

O'Neill's career allows us to conclude that we should not take him less seriously than we do, for his struggles with form and content were singularly intense and imaginative. More than any other writer in the American theatre he endeavored to give range and significance to the drama, which had previously been mostly a narrowly commercial enterprise. This endeavor alone would justify our sense of indebtedness to him and our readiness to place him in the company of the European theatrical pioneers. But there is another, less easily definable, quality that distinguishes O'Neill. Almost alone among our professional playwrights, he possessed a sense of integrity and self-immolating artistry that he never betrayed or even rationed.

O'NEILL AS A TRAGEDIAN

Moving darkly through the maze of the modern world, O'Neill, in his maturity, refused to be comforted by the material enticements of modern society. He accepted no solace from Marxist movements that powerfully attracted many of his fellow writers and attracted him briefly, too, in his youth. He accepted no assurances from the status quo either.

Another way of describing O'Neill's compulsion to wrestle with the angel—and O'Neill was one of the most compelled of modern playwrights—is to say that he was loyal to a tragic sense of life. He was a natural tragedian, though it is possible to question whether any particular play of his quite lived up to traditional high standards of tragedy, and though his forte was more tragicality than tragedy. But even if we agree with critics who believe his work, in lacking poetry and elevation, falls short of tragedy, we cannot legitimately deny his work tragic ambience. Above all, we must grant the integrity of his despair.

Although a frequently amiable person whose sense of humor (and it was often sturdy, even raffish) has been insufficiently acknowledged, O'Neill could never abide complacency. In the interview he gave to the press on the eve of the prêmiere of *The Iceman Cometh*, produced by the Theatre Guild in September, 1946, he reaffirmed his position by calling the United States the "greatest failure" in the world. The reason was "the everlasting game of trying to possess your own soul by possessing something outside of it, too," and America with its immense resources had been especially tempted to play that game. "This was really said in the Bible much better," he added. "We are the greatest example of 'for what shall it profit a man if he shall gain the whole world and lose his own soul?' We had so much and could have gone either way. . . ." O'Neill proceeded to enlarge his indictment to include the whole human race, concluding that, "if humanity failed to appreciate the secret of happiness contained in that simple sentence," it was time to "dump" the human race "down the nearest drain and let the ants have a chance."

O'Neill produced an impression of greatness by virtue of the absolute demands he made upon life and by an acute awareness of humanity's failures. His aim was to make the theatre express a Luciferian aspiration exceeded in some of his plays only by his sense of calamity that amounted to a Satanic sense of damnation. O'Neill is one of the few Faustians of modern literature . . . for whom damnation is a psychological reality rather than a convenient religious fiction.

It is true that O'Neill sometimes appears to be aiming too consciously at greatness. In the pursuit of magnitude he falls into some errors of taste and tact and tends to pile up his catastrophic situations and to schematize his dramatic conceptions—witness such ambitiously conceived pieces as *Strange Interlude* and *Mourning Becomes Electra*. But apparently the labor in his work had to *show* before the work could be impressive at all. He is not the man for finesse; his temperament appears to have had little use for it. Whenever there is truth or depth of experience in the plays it is futile to wish that he had composed them less repetitively and insistently. Their emotional power is bound up with their massiveness.

O'Neill's raw talent may embarrass his admirers, but it tends to reduce his detractors to impotence once they leave the library. In recent decades he presented the English-speaking commercial theatre with extreme challenges offered by only one other playwright, Sean O'Casey. O'Neill made the theatre rise to both his reasonable and unreasonable expectations. Intent upon having his say regardless of consequences to dramatic form or length, O'Neill became one of those rare playwrights with whom the practical theatre has been compelled to come to terms. There have been such writers in every theatrical period that has had some claim to significance. . . .

ALIENATION IN O'NEILL'S WORK

We do not come close enough to O'Neill's particular genius until we realize that it is obsessed with damnation. The anguish of alienation so pronounced in his work is far less conspicuous in the tragedies of Sophocles, Shakespeare, and Racine. They possessed the inestimable balm of great poetry, but this undeniably great gift is not the sole reason for their power to radiate light as well as heat and to attain a healing power rarely discernible in O'Neill. The point is that, unlike O'Neill, they were profoundly affirmative. After the 1920 production of *Beyond the Horizon* the elder O'Neill said to his son, "Are you trying to send your audience home to commit suicide?" There was a basis to the question.

Pessimism and the tragic spirit (which is ultimately affirmative) are at war in the works of O'Neill. In the canon there are plays, such as *The Iceman Cometh*, in which the playwright seems to put a premium on desperation, or, as in *A Moon for the Misbegotten*, to become prodigal with misery. But though he appears to have the Jacobean playwrights' taste for morbidity, he was usually more inclined to be mordant than morbid in his commentary on life, and his manner was chiefly one of a determined reaction against the optimism of shallow people breezily at ease in Zion. "Sure I'll write about happiness," he declared in an interview in 1922, "if I can happen to meet up with that luxury," and he went on to maintain that he found a compensating exaltation in writing tragedy. "A work of art," he said, "is always happy; all else is unhappy." But all these qualifications cannot quite remove an impression of incompleteness produced by much of his work. It is an incompleteness of tragedy, reflecting an incompleteness in the playwright himself.

O'Neill expresses a keen sense of loss quite aside from the usual tragic awareness of the misery of human life. It is hardly a secret that his special sense of desolation was associated with the loss of faith on the part of an introspective man who was born and reared a Catholic. A determined individualist unable to attach himself to the social causes that won the allegiance of many intellectuals in his time, he did not discover compensatory convictions. O'Neill gave continual evidence of traumatic experience in his youth, and the loss of religious faith was an important part of it; he makes much of the problem in *Dynamo* and *Days Without End*. We find in his work a keen sense of loss of connection—of connection with God, nature, society, family, father. O'Neill's ambivalence is certainly no longer a secret. He set it down, dramatizing its source in the family situation with rough tenderness and candor when he wrote *Long Day's Journey into Night.* This play, written late in his career, is explicit about ambivalences projected and symbolized in earlier plays. Here he was a characteristically modern dramatist, a divided man who was acutely aware of the division not only in himself but in his fellow men. Like his favorite modern playwright Strindberg, O'Neill made division itself the subject of his plays. In them he tried to master the division he found in human nature and in the human condition, and because this was no easy enterprise he was doomed to repeat the effort constantly.

Had O'Neill been a shallow man he might have settled for small satisfactions, had he been an essentially irreligious man he might not have been concerned with lack of faith, had he been an unloving man he might have been content with the gregariousness that passes for love among low-voltage individuals. The tensions in his work are nearly always connected with his struggle against alienation. The secret of his dramatic intensity is to be found not in his theatricality but in his rebellion and anger, in an inability to resign himself to an arid view and way of life. He could not be at ease in a world without God, without love, and without trust in life.

O'Neill's Accomplishments

Normand Berlin

Professor Normand Berlin defends O'Neill as a compassionate writer who uplifted and stretched American drama from escapist entertainment to serious theater. He pushed traditional boundaries of playwriting and opened new approaches to theater. His work included both American and European traditions to give his plays a cultural richness. Berlin argues that of all O'Neill's accomplishments, his most profound is his ability to move an audience emotionally by effectively dramatizing themes that deal with fundamental human concerns. O'Neill's vision as a tragic writer covers a broad range of subject matter, techniques, interests, and philosophy; as a playwright, Berlin finds O'Neill is uncategorizable.

Normand Berlin is a professor of English at the University of Massachusetts, Amherst. He is the author of *Thomas Sackville* and *The Base String: The Underworld in Elizabethan Drama*. He also contributes articles to numerous professional journals.

O'Neill's death on 27 November 1953 produced a few obituaries and appreciations by drama critics and academicians, surprisingly few in the light of his significant contribution to American drama and his worldwide reputation. The muted and minimal response seemed to suggest that O'Neill, the outstanding and successful dramatist back in the twenties and thirties, was not a dramatist for all seasons. Then, three years after his death, with the Jose Quintero productions of *The Iceman Cometh* and *Long Day's Journey Into Night* and with the publication of the posthumous plays of the fifties, O'Neill was rediscovered, and the revival of interest in the man and his work continued through the sixties and seventies. Judging from the enormous output of books and articles on O'Neill, from the many Ph.D. and MA theses written in universities, from the number of college courses on O'Neill alone, from the unavoidable inclusion of O'Neill in college survey courses on modern drama, and from the many productions of O'Neill's plays throughout America and the world (although not as many in America as so important a dramatist deserves), O'Neill has become a respectable classic, perhaps acquiring some of the academic encrustedness that the phrase brings with it, but a classic that continues to excite students of the drama in a surprisingly direct way. In a panel discussion on O'Neill, recorded in the *New York Theatre Review* (March 1978), Julius Novick, critic for the *Village Voice* and also a teacher, reported that 'students are interested in O'Neill in a way that they're not interested in any other playwright. I find that they make a kind of personal connection with him that they make with nobody else.' . . .

O'NEILL'S STATUS AS A DRAMATIST

Like all giants, O'Neill has blemishes that seem more gross precisely because he is a giant. Whatever his faults—and these will continue to be acknowledged and discussed and disputed—some clear and indisputable summarizing assertions can be made about O'Neill's accomplishments and status and dramatic art. First, O'Neill made American drama a *serious* endeavor. Before O'Neill American theatre was usually escapist entertainment; after O'Neill the phrase 'American drama' took on significance. Dramatists were able to aim high and treat serious subjects in a serious manner. This is his most important contribution to the history of American drama. One could pinpoint specific ways in which O'Neill influenced later dramatists. (Some examples: O'Neill's Yank Smith is the model for many strong inarticulate characters in later American drama; the line from O'Neill's hairy ape to Tennessee Williams's Stanley Kowalski is a direct one, as is the line from O'Neill's *Desire Under the Elms* to *Streetcar Named Desire* in the treatment of desire. O'Neill's expressionistic technique in *The Emperor Jones* and *The Hairy Ape* surely influenced Elmer Rice's *The Adding Machine* and Arthur Miller's *Death of a Salesman*. Miller's play also benefited from O'Neill's use of removable walls in *Desire Under the Elms*.) But no specific influence on the works of later dramatists is as important as the larger influence of O'Neill's independent and aspiring example. He took his art seriously; he challenged his audience; he was totally committed to his work— and he thereby paved the way for others, from the twenties on. He made American drama important, and allowed America to compete with the Europeans in that art form. In short, he gave his integrity to the profession he chose. He would be an artist or nothing, he wrote to George Pierce Baker; therefore, for O'Neill drama would be an art or nothing.

O'NEILL'S EXPERIMENTATION

Second, O'Neill stretched the boundaries of his medium, in the themes and characters he chose to dramatize and in the techniques he used. He was America's boldest experimenter, and he opened up new possibilities of theatre. To this day, no other American playwright approaches his technical inventiveness. His was the first important use of expressionism in America, as well as the first important use of realism. His was the most imaginative use of sound and light and gesture and movement and setting, all highly emotive. He was a master craftsman who had an instinctive understanding of the theatre and what an audience wants. He was able to make demands on that audience in the face of opposition from producers and directors. He took risks, and usually his audience went along with him, responding to his sincerity of purpose.

O'NEILL'S CULTURAL TRADITION

Third, O'Neill belongs to both an American tradition and a European tradition. Raleigh makes a clear case for O'Neill's cultural roots in America, not only his inheritance of his father's nineteenth-century theatre, but also his exploration of the American experience, an exploration resembling the writings of 'classical American literature of the nineteenth century', which includes the work of Edgar Allan Poe, Nathaniel Hawthorne, Herman Melville, Ralph Waldo Emerson, Henry David Thoreau, Henry Adams, and Walt Whitman. Indeed, O'Neill's depiction of New England Puritanism, his interest in Transcendentalism, his sense of the sea, his interest in the lower elements of society, and his emphasis on aloneness, on the solitary figure up against society, most important perhaps, his general sense of fatality in human lives, the dark side of human existence—these are part of his inheritance as an *American* writer. But Europe also gave him, as it gave

America, some of its cultural wealth—in philosophy, psychology, literature and drama. O'Neill acknowledged the importance of Strindberg and Nietzsche to his art and thought and mission, and we can add to those giants others, like Freud, Jung, Marx, Shakespeare, Ibsen, Shaw, Chekhov, Synge and Conrad, to name just a few, and perhaps most important, the Greek dramatists, who provided O'Neill with some of the basic ingredients of tragedy, and who allowed him to believe that writing drama was the noblest human endeavor. (The Orient, through some American writers and directly, also influenced O'Neill's thought.) What O'Neill inherited he made his own, sifting it through his distinctive perspective, through his personal experiences.

O'NEILL'S EMOTIONAL APPEAL

Fourth, O'Neill's appeal is primarily emotional; he knows how to move an audience. He always believed, as he stated in 1922, that 'our emotions are a better guide than our thoughts. Our emotions are instinctive. They are the result not only of our individual experiences but of the experiences of the whole human race, back through the ages.' O'Neill's emphasis on the emotions helps to explain his feeling of closeness to Nietzsche, whose philosophy strongly acknowledged the emotional, nonrational, rapturous, Dionysian side of man. (It also helps to explain the importance of drunkenness in O'Neill's plays, because intoxication can touch the truth of life more easily than can the rational mind.) O'Neill himself felt deeply what he wrote; here the autobiographical pressure makes itself felt. He ransacked his memory, he was intrinsically connected to his Irish and Catholic roots, he wrote out his agony and guilt, he used the theatre as a vehicle for remembrance and self-analysis and self-forgiveness. This *personal* involvement in what he writes cannot be measured in any exact way and cannot be an important part of the analysis of a particular play—but it is there, serving as an emotional prod to the writer himself, and somehow infusing his best plays with *feeling*. O'Neill was able to use the most objective of verbal arts to mirror his personal agonies. One can say that O'Neill's Drama is Theatre working on Memory. He was essentially a private dramatist who—by dealing with his own fears and guilt, and by manipulating the scenic means at his disposal—uncannily managed to touch the private agonies of his viewers.

O'NEILL'S PROFOUND THEMES

Another reason for his emotional appeal is the emotional quality of the themes he dramatizes—love, death, frustration, illusion, fate—themes that touch the very nature of existence, the common and continually profound *interests* in life when man is thinking and feeling, especially feeling. O'Neill himself affirmed in unequivocal terms his pursuit of the *truth* of man's existence as measured by *feeling*.

> I intend to use whatever I can make my own, to write about anything under the sun in any manner that fits or can be invented to fit the subject. And I shall never be influenced by any consideration but one: Is it the truth as I know it—or, better still, feel it?

In 1924 he said, 'I write of life as I see it.' Three years earlier he stated: 'I just set down what I feel in terms of life and let the facts speak whatever language they may to my audience.' The truth of life as he sees it and feels it is the essential beginning in his process of composition; language and form and technical devices follow from that. It is that 'truth' which gives his plays the emotional resonances that affect his audience. He believed that 'truth usually goes deep. So it reaches you through your emotions.' To use Yank Smith's words, 'Dis ting's in your inside.' In a conversation with Joseph Wood Krutch, O'Neill gave clear expression to the religious nature of his quest for truth. 'Most modern plays are concerned with the relation between man and man, but that does not interest me at all. I am interested only in the relation between man and God.' Since O'Neill believed that 'the old God' was dead and a 'new One' was not created by 'science and materialism', his investigation of the relationship between man and God inevitably led to dark thoughts about man's precarious and lonely position, his inability to 'belong', even the absurdity of man's trapped condition.

A PLETHORA OF THEMES

However, that he saw the relationship between man and God as the important one to write about should not lead us to think of him *exclusively* in those terms. O'Neill wrote a great number of plays, which display a wide range of subject-matter, interest, character and technique. (After destroying a large number of manuscripts, for one reason or another, O'Neill still left us forty-nine published plays, about half of which are full length or more than full length.) Small wonder, then, that his plays have been labeled not only 'religious', in keeping with his stated general intent, but also 'philosophical', 'mystical', 'ritualistic', 'psychological', 'historical', 'social', and 'biographical', with O'Neill himself called a realist, a naturalist, a romanticist, and a mystic, to name only the most common designations. Obviously, no one adjective or noun can contain so prolific and so large a dramatist, although each label or combination of labels— depending on the particular play under discussion—can be applied to him in one way or another.

O'NEILL'S TRAGIC VISION

The single designation that we can attach to him with the greatest assurance is that O'Neill is a dramatist of the emotions. And the single vision that informs most of his work is the tragic vision, placing him in the company of his admired Greek dramatists and in the company of Shakespeare and Chekhov and Beckett, all of whom occupy common tragic ground. O'Neill, very early in his career, recognized what that ground was. In 1921 O'Neill said, 'To me, the tragic alone has that significant beauty which is truth.' And in 1945, after his work was over, he made the important statement that he was

> always conscious of the Force behind—Fate, God, our biological past creating our present, whatever one calls it—Mystery certainly—and of the one eternal tragedy of Man in his glorious, self-destructive struggle to make the Force express him instead of being, as an animal is, an infinitesimal incident in its expression.

The celebration of mystery, the pressure of the force behind, the sense of fated frustration and sadness, the nobility of man's struggle or endurance, the dramatization of the question mark of our lives, the knowledge that no answers to life's important questions can ever be found—these are the characteristics of tragedy that allow us to talk of a tragic tradition, of which O'Neill is a powerful representative. Larry Slade is uttering O'Neill's sentiments when he says he feels 'damned' because 'the questions multiply for you until in the end it's all question and no answer.' And O'Neill himself, when discussing *The Hairy Ape*, said that 'we are all sick of answers that don't answer. *The Hairy Ape* at least faces the simple truth that, being what we are . . . there just is no answer.' With such statements, O'Neill places himself on the precarious curve of the question mark. In his best plays O'Neill presents directly to our *emotions*—without the theatrical devices that call attention to themselves as devices, like masks and internal monologues, but always with the stage image carefully designed, always with form serving his theme, always prodded by the truth as he feels it—the dark meanderings of our lives, the palpable frustration and sadness of our condition, the sense of being caught in a net, the secrecy of the cause.

O'NEILL AND THE TRAGIC TRADITION

In an interview with journalist Malcolm Mollan in the January 22, 1922, Philadelphia Public Ledger, *reprinted in Barrett H. Clark's* Eugene O'Neill: The Man and His Plays, *O'Neill, when asked about writing "happy-ending" plays, outlines his commitment to writing tragedy.*

Sure I'll write about happiness if I can happen to meet up with that luxury, and find it sufficiently dramatic and in harmony with any deep rhythm in life. But happiness is a word. What does it mean? Exaltation; an intensified feeling of the significant worth of man's being and becoming? Well, if it means that—and not a mere smirking contentment with one's lot—I know there is more of it in one real tragedy than in all the happy-ending plays ever written. It's mere present-day judgment to think of tragedy as unhappy! The Greeks and the Elizabethans knew better. They felt the tremendous lift to it. It roused them spiritually to a deeper understanding of life. Through it they found release from the petty consideration of everyday existence. They saw their lives ennobled by it.

At the core of everything O'Neill wrote is a burning intensity that eludes description or definition or analysis. It comes from a subterranean cavern of his soul, one might even say a hellish cavern, as if O'Neill looked with his dark piercing eyes into a place where others are forbidden to look and was compelled to report what he saw, always knowing (feeling) that what he saw could never be reported accurately, that the darkly inexpressible could never be expressed. He recognized his inadequacy as witness. Edmund Tyrone is talking for O'Neill: 'I couldn't touch what I tried to tell you just now. I just stammered. That's the best I'll ever do, I mean if I live. Well, it will be faithful realism, at least. Stammering is the native eloquence of us fog people.'

Yet, what O'Neill managed to 'touch' places him among the major dramatists of the world. Nietzsche warned, 'Gaze not too long into the abyss or the abyss will gaze into you.' O'Neill did not follow his favorite philosopher's advice. He gazed too long. That his dramatic art allows us to *feel* something of what he saw testifies to the challenge he set for himself and to his astonishing accomplishment.

CHAPTER 3

Analysis of Specific Plays

Expressionism in
The Emperor Jones

Virginia Floyd

With *The Emperor Jones*, O'Neill moves away from
realistic drama and begins an experimental approach
to play production that revolutionizes American theater
in the 1920s. Virginia Floyd explores O'Neill's use of
setting, lighting, and sound to create an expressionistic
play that explores emotions and psychological tension.
Floyd argues that the settings in *The Emperor Jones* are
not realistic scenes, but dreamlike images played out in
the distorted interior life of the main character. Light,
for example, is used to project Jones's states of mind.
The bright lighting that symbolizes Jones's early clarity
of mind dims to shadowy moonlight and finally darkness as his sanity diminishes. Throughout the course
of the play, a low vibrating tom-tom beats at an accelerating pace as Jones descends into madness.

Floyd suggests that Jones's journey offers the audience an
unsettling look at the plight of the American blacks facing
white oppression during the 1920s and 1930s. Jones, who
emulates the ways of whites, plays out two important ideas:
the Faustian theme and the religious quest. Floyd argues that
Jones, like Faust, sells his soul for material possessions and
not only loses himself but also his God. Only through his
suffering and death does he finally find redemption.

Virginia Floyd is a professor at Bryant College, Providence.
Her works include *Eugene O'Neill: The Unfinished Plays,
Eugene O'Neill at Work: Newly Released Ideas for Plays,* and
Eugene O'Neill: A World View.

The new O'Neill, the craftsman who was to revolutionize the
American theater in the 1920s in his experimental period,
emerges in *The Emperor Jones*. In it, the author moves
beyond anything he had previously attempted in an effort to

integrate form and subject matter. He blends expressionism with realism to dramatize the tragedy of the deposed despot Brutus Jones, whose flight for freedom, which becomes a personal quest for self-identity, takes him to his death.

O'NEILL'S USE OF EXPRESSIONISM

O'Neill's use of expressionism in *The Emperor Jones* had two effects: first, it brought him into the mainstream of the European experimental theatrical movement; second, it established his international reputation. Directors in Sweden, Germany, and other countries on the continent took note of the young American and began producing his dramas. O'Neill claims not to have been influenced by the European movement. *Jones*, he states, "was written long before I had ever heard of Expressionism." He apparently had not read German expressionists, such as Georg Kaiser and Ernst Toller, before beginning *The Emperor Jones* and probably came to the new mode by way of Strindberg, who also provided the impetus for Central European dramatists. There is a marked similarity between the flashing dream sequences showing Brutus Jones moving back into his personal and racial past and those depicting the Daughter of Indra journeying forward into her mortal life in Strindberg's *A Dream Play.*

The Emperor Jones relies primarily on expressionistic settings for its effectiveness. The drama begins and ends with realistic scenes in the present, but its six intervening scenes are played out in the hero's wild, distorted mind, as his convoluted trip through the forest takes him back further and further into the past. Reality becomes distorted fragments filtered through Jones's consciousness as he enacts his thoughts in dreamlike reveries. The first scene is set in a spacious room in the Emperor's palace "on an island in the West Indies as yet not self-determined by white Marines." Everything in the room—walls, tiles, pillars—is white, an appropriate blank background for the statement-making "dazzling, eye-smiting scarlet" throne of the arrogant, brutal despot. It is late afternoon, the last day of the Emperor's reign.

CHARACTERIZATION

Jones, a powerfully built, middle-aged black man, enters. His face displays "an underlying strength of will, a hardy, self-reliant confidence in himself that inspires respect. His eyes are alive with a keen, cunning intelligence. In manner he is shrewd, suspicious, evasive." He wears an outlandish uniform: a blue jacket decorated with brass buttons and gold braid and bright red trousers with a light blue stripe down the side. A pearl-handled revolver in its holster and patent leather boots with brass spurs resemble the gear of an outlaw of the American frontier and clash with the attempt to ape the finery of European monarchs. "Yet there is something not altogether ridiculous about his grandeur. He has a way of carrying it out."

With Jones is Smithers, a white Cockney trader about forty years old. His "naturally pasty face" has been transformed by the sun to a "sickly yellow, and native rum has painted his pointed nose to a starling red." His expression is one of "unscrupulous meanness, cowardly and dangerous." He is clearly portrayed as the black man's inferior. Jones, in his two years on the island, has learned the language of the natives and taught some of them English. Smithers has been there ten years and still cannot communicate verbally with them. The former forged his way from a lowly stowaway, after his escape from an American jail, to emperor. He had been Smithers's employee, doing, as he says, "de dirty work fo you—and most o' de brain work." During a revolution Jones had seized power after surviving an assassination attempt by Lem, a native chief. When Lem's hired killer, standing only ten feet away, failed to shoot Jones, the people fell to their knees as though it were a "miracle out o' de Bible." Jones told the superstitious natives that only a silver bullet could kill him. His revolver contains five lead bullets and one "silver baby," "his rabbit's foot," which he intends to use to kill himself "when de time comes."

Jones has exploited his subjects and plundered the island, using the lessons he learned "listenin' to de white quality talk" during his ten years as a Pullman porter. He has hidden his wealth in a foreign bank and plotted the route he will follow to escape through the forest while pretending to be hunting. He plans to make his way to the forest's edge and to travel through the woods to the coast, where a French gunboat will take him to Martinique. "And dere I is safe wid a mighty big bankroll in my jeans.". . .

The low, vibrating sound of a tom-tom is heard. "It starts at a rate exactly corresponding to normal pulse beat—72 to

THE ORIGIN OF *THE EMPEROR JONES*

In an interview recorded in the November 9, 1924, New York World, *O'Neill discusses the origin of the drumbeat that permeates* The Emperor Jones. *Excerpts from the interview are reprinted in* Eugene O'Neill: The Man and His Plays *by Barrett H. Clark.*

One day I was reading of the religious feasts in the Congo and the uses to which the drum is put there: how it starts at a normal pulse and is slowly intensified until the heartbeat of everyone present corresponds to the frenzied beat of the drum. There was an idea and an experiment. How would this sort of thing work on an audience in a theater? The effect of the tropical forest on the human imagination was honestly come by. It was the result of my own experience while prospecting for gold in Spanish Honduras.

the minute—and continues at a gradually accelerating rate from this point uninterruptedly to the very end of the play." According to the trader, the natives are "'oldin' their 'eathen religious service." "They'll 'ave their pet devils and ghosts 'roundin' after you." Jones is contemptuous of the natives' ceremony. "As a member in good standin' o' de Baptist Church," he feels protected against their "devil spells and charms." Reminded that he has ignored that church for the past years, Jones reasons: "It don't git me nothin' to do missionary work for de Baptist Church." The scene closes with Jones's departure for the woods "with studied carelessness."

TECHNICAL DEVICES USED EXPRESSIONISTICALLY

The mood of the play shifts in the next six scenes as Jones makes his way through the jungle into the past and self-awareness. Here the technical devices of expressionism—lighting, setting, sound—are used to project the Emperor's visions, to reveal his state of mind. The scenes form one prolonged dramatic monologue, part dialogue when he addresses his "ha'nts," part soliloquy when he talks to himself.

In *Long Day's Journey into Night* O'Neill equates the weather and Mary Tyrone's mind; as the fog increases so too does her drug-induced haziness. In *The Emperor Jones* he achieves the same effect using lighting, going from the blazing sunlight of the first scene, where the hero's mind is clear, to the moonlight "merged into a veil of bluish mist" in the seventh scene, where fear undermines his sanity. It is not yet dark in the second scene when Jones reaches the Great Forest. He eyes the deep wall of darkness before him with a sense of foreboding and tries to cheer himself with the expectation of food. He searches in vain, however, for the "tin box o' grub" he has hidden previously. From the forest creep black, shapeless "Little Formless Fears" with glittering eyes. They emit a "low mocking laughter" and squirm menacingly toward him. Terrified, he takes out his revolver and fires, sending the creatures back to the woods. The power of the gun gives him self-confidence and he boldly enters the forest.

The moon in the third scene casts an "eerie glow" on the small triangular clearing Jones has reached. The blackness of the woods resembles "an encompassing barrier." The tom-tom beats a trifle louder now. Jeff, a middle-aged black man in a Pullman porter's uniform, crouches in the rear of the triangular space, casting dice with the "mechanical movements of an automaton." Jones freezes in fear. "Day tol' me you done died from dat razor cut I gives you." In his frenzy, he pulls out his revolver and fires at the specter and then plunges into the underbrush. . . .

Whereas Jones retreats into his personal past in the first expressionistic scenes, in the next three he regresses into the collective consciousness of his race, the *Spiritus Mundi* William Butler Yeats speaks of in "The Second Coming." In Scene 5 the moon outlines a circular clearing in the woods, Jones throws himself on his knees and pleads: "Lawd Jesus, heah my prayer!" A confession of his three crimes follows: the two murders and the theft of all he could extort from the natives. Fervently, he prays to be delivered.

A crowd, dressed in Southern costumes of the 1850s, converges on the clearing: planters, an auctioneer, a group of "young belles and dandies who have come to the slave-market for diversion." Their movements are "stiff, rigid, unreal, marionettish." A group of slaves is appraised by planters. Jones is forced to stand on the auction block. He glares with "raging hatred and fear" at the auctioneer and the planter who is buying him and fires two shots at them. Jones rushes off, maddened by fear and the progressively louder beat of the tom-tom. . . .

The Emperor Jones is the first of many attempts O'Neill made in the 1920s and 1930s to depict the plight of blacks in

America. Granted, Jones does exploit his own people. The narrated betrayal, however, is overshadowed by the dramatized examples of white oppression: the cruelty of the white guard to the chained convicts, the sale of human beings as slaves, the forced voyage on slave ships of innocent people uprooted from their African homes. O'Neill elaborates on all of these details in a projected work in 1927, "Bantu Boy," the full-length study of the life of one such victim. Like Jones, the central figure would endure harrowing treatment in America and finally makes his way back to his roots, in Africa, at the end.

THE FAUST THEME

A second dominant motif that emerged in the 1920s and is illustrated in *The Emperor Jones* is the Faust theme. Jones is a man who clearly has sold his soul for material possession: "I'se after de coin, an' I lays my Jesus on de shelf for de time bein'." The "debils" pursue him until he surrenders his soul in death. He commits his first crime, Jeff's murder, in a squabble over money and succumbs to greed and the lure of "white quality talk," assuming the role normally played by white oppressors as he exploits his black subjects. He expiates his crime later when he undergoes the demeaning experiences of his race, the humiliation on the auction block, the confinement in the hold of a slave ship crossing the Atlantic.

Somewhere along the route from porter to Emperor, as he emulates the ways of whites, Jones loses sight of who he is. He rejects his black identity and heritage and scorns the garments of the natives, the loincloth worn by Lem. The royal trappings become the embodiment of Jones's pseudo-self; by shedding them piece by piece, he strips away the layers of veneer of white society. After witnessing the historical tragedies of his race, he is reduced to a tattered breechcloth. Appropriately, the seventh scene is set in Africa. Having denied his cultural roots, Jones must make amends there.

RELIGIOUS QUEST

Jones's long night's journey into the past is a religious quest as well as a personal search for identity. During the assimilation process in white America, Jones lost not only his black culture and values but also his native beliefs. The only remaining traces are his superstitions. He has adopted the God the white man fashioned into his own likeness, yet he abandoned even this God in his pursuit of wealth. His own conscience and the witch doctor pronounce him guilty and condemn him to be sacrificed to the crocodile god. At the moment that Jones begins his penitential crawl toward the open jaws and prays for deliverance, he remembers the silver bullet. Ironically, the crocodile god proves to be his undoing. Shooting it brings him death, for the noise alerts Lem and his men to his location. The death of the crocodile god sends the witch doctor hurrying away. Jones lies with "his face to the ground, his arms outstretched," in the symbolic position of the crucified Christ, suggesting that he has, through his suffering, atoned and found redemption.

The Emperor Jones was a landmark drama, not only in conception but also in production: a black actor, Charles Gilpin, was permitted for the first time to enact the leading role in a New York drama. The play was a critical and popular success, and the critics attributed considerable credit to Gilpin for his brilliant portrayal of Jones. Years later, in an interview in 1946, O'Neill said: "As I look back now on all my work, I can honestly say there was only one actor who carried out every notion of a character I had in mind. That actor was Charles Gilpin." *The Emperor Jones* signaled a coming of age of the American theater. Its triumph convinced O'Neill that audiences would accept experimental works and plays focusing on the controversial racial problem in America. The two elements, technique and the until-then taboo topic, would merge and emerge two years later in *All God's Chillun Got Wings.*

The Quest for God in *Desire Under the Elms*

Roger Asselineau

Roger Asselineau claims O'Neill's playwriting was a compulsion that helped him deal with loneliness, emptiness, and despair. According to Asselineau, *Desire Under the Elms* is a philosophical play that reflects O'Neill's quest for God and religion. In the play the three main characters act on their instincts, like animals. They are trapped by social, moral, environmental, and psychological circumstances. Asselineau argues that although the characters are not free they can save their souls and transcend their animal state through passion. For O'Neill this passion is God, a spontaneous, unselfish, amoral, and cosmic life force that permeates nature and has the power to soften lonesomeness and offer a glimpse of fulfillment and hope. This is the "desire" that flows through the "elms" of nature. The love of Abbie and Eben moves them to this life impulse but, by contrast, Ephraim Cabot remains steadfastly alone with his puritanical God of repression, hardness, and guilt.

Roger Asselineau is a professor of American literature at Sorbonne, University of Paris. His works include *The Evolution of Walt Whitman* and *The Transcendentalist Constant in American Literature.* He is a contributor to various periodicals.

Though to all appearances O'Neill was primarily a playwright and an experimenter with dramatic forms who never considered himself a thinker, he was in fact desperately trying to express "something" in all his plays. He chose drama as a medium, but, for all his interest in technique, he never considered it an end in itself, but rather a means to live by

Excerpted from "*Desire Under the Elms:* A Phase of Eugene O'Neill's Philosophy" by Roger Asselineau, in *Festschrift für Rudolf Stamm*, edited by Eduard Kolb and Jörg Hasler (Bern: A. Francke, 1969). Reprinted by permission of the publisher.

proxy a certain number of problems which obsessed him. In *Lazarus Laughed*, he speaks of men as "those haunted heroes." Actually this is less a definition of mankind than a description of himself. He composed plays because he *had* to write in order to liberate himself and exorcise ghosts. It was a compulsion. The result was plays because of his environment, because his father was an actor and he was an "enfant de la balle," but it might have been novels just as well, and he would probably have written better novels than plays, for he was constantly hampered by the limitations of the stage. In his case literary creation was not a gratuitous activity, but an intense imaginative experience, an *"Erlebnis."* He lived it. It was a passionate answer to the problems which tormented him with excruciating strength. This is no mere figure of speech. He roamed the world for years in search of a solution, trying to find a remedy for his fundamental despair, giving up the comfort and security of family life and nearly losing his health and life in the process.

After his wandering years, his *Wanderjahre,* when his health broke down and he was obliged to bring his restless comings-and-goings to a close, he went on exploring the world in imagination, not as a dilettante or a tourist in the realms of thought, but as a passionate pilgrim in quest of a shrine at which to worship. Though brought up a Roman Catholic, he lost his faith as an adolescent. Yet his nature abhorred this spiritual vacuum and he ardently looked for a substitute ever after. His religious faith was killed by rationalism and scientific materialism, but the restlessness and violence of his quest for a personal religion sprang from no coldly rational intellect.

Each of his plays is thus not only an experiment in craftsmanship, but also an attempt to find God or at least some justification for the flagrant inconsistencies of the human condition. His interest was less in psychology than in metaphysics. He said so himself in a letter to Joseph Wood Krutch: "Most modern plays are concerned with the relation between man and man, but that does not interest me at all. I am interested only in the relation between man and God."

In spite of its apparent dramatic directness therefore, *Desire Under the Elms* is essentially, like his other plays, a philosophical tragedy about man and God rather than a naturalistic chunk of life depicting the mores of a bunch of clumsy New England rustics.

ANIMAL NATURE OF MAN

Reduced to essentials in this very primitive setting man appears primarily as an animal. The first specimens whom we have a chance to observe when the curtain rises, Eben and especially Simeon and Peter, look like oxen, eat, work and behave like a team of oxen, and feel tied up to the other animals of the farm by bonds of brotherhood: ". . . the cows knows us . . . An' the hosses, an' pigs, an' chickens . . . They knows us like brothers—and likes us" (Part I, scene 4). They obey their instincts blindly and think only of drinking, eating and fornicating. Their lust is quite literally bestial as is shown by Eben's account of his visit to Min: "I begun t'beller like a calf an' cuss at the same time . . . an' she got scared, an' I just grabbled holt an' tuk her" (Part I, scene 3). When Abbie courts Eben, the scene is not much different. She kisses him greedily and at first he submits dumbly, but soon, after returning her kisses he hurls her away from him and, O'Neill tells us, "they stand speechless and breathless, panting like two animals" (Part II, scene 2).

These inarticulate, animal-like creatures differ from their dumb brothers in only one respect (but it is hardly an improvement): they are possessed with the mania of owning things, whether gold or land. They all crave for money or title-deeds. In short, they bear a strong family likeness to Swift's Yahoos. They have only one redeeming feature: an embryonic sense of beauty which makes them exclaim "purty" in a rather monotonous manner whenever they notice the beauty of their surroundings. The only exception is the sheriff, who at the very end of the play passes very matter-of-fact and anti-climactic comments on the salable value of the farm while Eben and Abbie admire the beauty of the sunrise.

MAN TRAPPED BY CIRCUMSTANCE

Far from being a free agent, man is thus by and large the slave of his instincts and O'Neill here revives the old Calvinistic dogma of predestination. As early as his very first play, *The Web*, of the transparent title, he attempted to show that man is caught in a web of circumstances, a web that is not of his own weaving. At the end of *The Web*, O'Neill tells us that Rose, the prostitute, "seems to be aware of something in the room which none of the others can see—perhaps the personification of the ironic life force that has crushed her." In *Desire Under the Elms* Eben feels trapped in exactly the same way: "Each day," the stage directions inform us, "is a cage in which he finds himself trapped." He is indeed trapped by circumstances—tied up to that bleak New England farm which he somehow considers part of his mother, and he is also psychologically trapped by an all-powerful mother-complex which unknown to him determines his whole behavior towards his father as well as towards women in general. His temperament is wholly determined by his heredity: it is a combination of his mother's softness and lack of will, as his father again and again points out, and of his father's aggressiveness and obstinacy, as his two elder brothers repeatedly tell us: "he is a chip off the old block, the spitting image of his father. . . ."

As to Abbie, she is just as trapped as he is. When she enters the stage, we are warned that she has "the same unsettled, untamed, desperate quality which is so apparent in Eben." And shortly afterwards we learn that she "was a orphan early an' had t'wuk fur others in other folks' hums" and her first husband "turned out a drunken spreer" and got sick and died. She then felt free again only to discover that all she was free for was to work again "in other folks' hums, doin' other folks' wuk" till she had almost given up hope of ever doing her own work in her own home (Part I, scene 4).

Ephraim Cabot himself, for all his will-power and vigor, is caught in the same web as the others. His whole behavior is conditioned by his Puritan upbringing. He cannot think of anything but work, hard work on a barren New England farm. "*Laborare est orare*," Carlyle claimed, "work is worship." Ephraim Cabot is a degenerate Puritan. Work has ceased to be a form of worship for him, yet he believes in its virtue and absolute value because he has been brought up that way. He once tried to escape this self-imposed serfdom. Like many other New Englanders, he went West and in the broad meadows of the central plains found black soil as rich as gold, without a stone. He had only to plough and sow and then sit and smoke his pipe and watch things grow. He could have become a rich man and led an easy and idle life, but he preferred to give it up and return to his New England farm and to hard work on a stony soil, which proves the extraordinary strength of his Puritan compulsions. They practically deprived him of his freedom of choice.

So, at the start at least, the three major characters of *Desire Under the Elms* are not free. They bear psychological or moral chains. Consequently, they cannot be held responsible for their actions and Simeon with his peasant shrewdness is perfectly aware of it. When Eben accuses his father of killing his "Maw," Simeon retorts: "No one never kills nobody. It's allus somethin' that's the murderer" (Part I, scene 2). "Somethin'," that is to say one of those mysterious things which impel men to act this way or that, whether they like it or not, whether they are aware of it or not. This is a modified form of Puritan pessimism: all men are sinners in the clutches of Satan—or of God who is always "nagging his sheep to sin" (Part I, scene 4), the better to punish them afterwards, always ready to smite his undutiful sons with his worst curse.

THE REDEEMING POWER OF PASSION

How can a man save his soul under such circumstances? Though, theoretically, O'Neill's approach is strictly non-theological and he is not concerned with the problem of salvation, he is constantly obsessed with it all the same and in this particular play, he gives it a Nietzschean[1] answer: passion. Passion alone, he suggests, can enable man to transcend his animal nature. He repeatedly exalts the purity and trans-figuring power of love. Eben's passion for Abbie which at first is mere lust soon becomes love—and there is a difference in kind between the two. The passage from lust to love is similar to the transmutation of lead into gold. Whereas lust, which is tied to the body, is finite and transient, love, which transcends the body, is infinite and eternal. Abbie kills her infant son to prove her love to Eben, and at the end of scene 3 of Part III proclaims that her love for Eben will never change, whatever he does to her. The play ends on an apotheosis of love. The two lovers stand "looking up raptly in attitudes strangely aloof and devout" at the "purty" rising sun, which contrasts with the pallid setting sun that lit up the opening of the play, at a time when everything took place on the plane of coarse material things and lust.

Man can thus be redeemed by a great passion and save his soul and attain grandeur. The farm under the elms, which looked so sordid when the curtain rose, witnesses a sublime *dénouement* and at the end almost becomes one of those places where the spirit bloweth.

---

1. German philosopher, Friedrich

The reason for this extraordinary change is that, in Hamlet's words:

There are more things in heaven and earth . . .
Than are dreamt of in all [our] philosophy,

as Cabot again and again feels, for all his hardness and insensitivity: "They's thin's pokin' about in the dark—in the corners" (Part II, scene 2). "Even the music can't drive it out—somethin'. Ye kin feel it droppin' off the elums, climbin' up the roof, sneakin' down the chimney, pokin' in the corners. They's no peace in houses, they's no rest livin' with folks. Somethin's always livin' with ye. . ." (Part III, scene 2).

GOD IN NATURE

What is that "somethin'" whose presence disturbs him? It is the "Desire" of the title—an irresistible life-force (somewhat similar to G.B. Shaw's[2]), which flows through the elms and through old Cabot himself sometimes, as when it makes him leave his farm in spring and go in search of a new wife. But it is especially powerful in Eben and Abbie. It is that thing which makes Eben look like a wild animal in captivity when he enters the stage and feel "inwardly unsubdued." It is quite impersonal and Eben refers to it in the neuter: "I kin feel it growin' in me—growin' an' growin'—till it'll bust out" (Part I, scene 2). It is the magnetic force which draws Eben to Abbie through walls and partitions (Part II, scene 2). It is Nature—and Abbie intones a hymn to her—or it—in her own inarticulate way when she presses Eben to yield to his passion: "Hain't the sun strong an' hot? Ye kin feel it burnin' into the earth—Nature—makin' thin's grow—bigger 'n' bigger—burnin' inside ye—makin' ye want t'grow—into somethin' else—till ye are jined with it—an' it's your'n—but it owns ye—too—an' makes ye grow bigger—like a tree—like them elums" (Part II, scene 1).

In short, the "Desire" which flows through the elms and drips from them and pervades everything under them is God—though the word is never used. It is not, however, the God of the Christians, but rather a dynamic, impersonal, pantheistic or panpsychistic deity present in all things, whether animate or inanimate, breaking barriers between individuals as in the case of Eben and Abbie, dissolving their lonesomeness and making them feel one. In a way it is a pagan God, a Dionysian deity, for it partly manifests itself in

2. Irish dramatist

the form of carnal desire. Under its influence, Eben and Cabot become inspired poets (in prose) and sing woman, the lovely incarnation of the soft and warm goddess of fertility and life: "She's like t'night, she's soft 'n' warm, her eyes kin wink like a star, her mouth's wa'm, her arms're wa'm. She smells like a wa'm plowed field, she's purty" (Part I, scene 2). "Yew air my Rose o' Sharon! Behold! yew air fair; yer eyes air doves; yer lips air like scarlet; yer two breasts air like two fawns; yer navel be like a round goblet; yer belly be like a heap o' wheat," exclaims old Cabot echoing chapters 4 and 7 of the Song of Solomon.

This omnipresent God is fundamentally a cosmic sexual urge, spontaneous, beautiful, unselfish and amoral. In this perspective the notion of sin becomes meaningless. "He was the child of our sin," says Eben of the baby, but Abbie proudly answers "as if defying God" (the God of the Christians): "I don't repent that sin. I ain't askin' God t'fergive that" (Part III, scene 4). The two lovers have gone back to the Garden of Eden from which Adam and Eve were expelled. They have become "Children of Adam," to take up Walt Whitman's phrase.

The life-force, the desire which circulates through the elms as well as through the *dramatis personae* is the very reverse of the God worshipped by Ephraim Cabot, which has the hardness and immobility of a stone—and the sterility of one (Part II, scene 2). His God is the God of repression and lonesomeness and hard work—the God humorously called up by Robert Frost in "Of the Stones of the Place" and to some extent a duplicate of Robinson Jeffers's anti-human God.

Abbie, on the contrary, recommends to yield to the life impulse, to let Nature speak at every hazard "without check with original energy." It is against nature, it is impious, she claims, to resist its will: "It's agin nature, Eben. Ye been fightin' yer nature ever since the day I come. . . ." (Part II, scene 1).

This is a combination of Nietzsche's Dionysian philosophy and Freudianism and in *Desire Under the Elms* it leads—in spite of the Dostoevskian quality of the *Crime and Punishment* situation at the end of the play—to an optimistic conclusion: the couple Eben-Abbie is not crushed by adverse circumstances. They have fulfilled themselves, they have fully lived and, far from being driven to despair by their trials, they are full of a strange "hopeless hope" when the curtain falls.

Race Relations in *All God's Chillun Got Wings*

John Henry Raleigh

Like many American writers, Eugene O'Neill was fascinated by the racial polarity in the United States. John Henry Raleigh maintains that O'Neill's play *All God's Chillun Got Wings* is one of the most serious and compassionate treatments of this theme ever written. Raleigh writes that the characters, particularly Jim and Ella, a black-white couple, cannot escape the racial state of mind imposed by society. Ella is unable to overcome her conditioned notion that whites are superior and Jim suffers the humiliations and frustrations of being black in a white culture. Raleigh concludes that in its full scope *All God's Chillun Got Wings* is about two human beings caught in a deterministic and tragic struggle to find happiness—a struggle they cannot win.

John Henry Raleigh is a professor emeritus of English literature at the University of California, Berkeley. His works include *Time, Place, and Idea* and *The Chronicle of Leopold and Molly Brown*. He is the editor of *Twentieth-Century Interpretations of "The Iceman Cometh."*

The classical O'Neill play about the American Negro, and one of the best on the subject, is *All God's Chillun Got Wings*, and since it is one of the most serious, compassionate, and profound artistic treatments of the racial problem in America ever written, comparable to *Huckleberry Finn* or *Pudd'nhead Wilson* or *The Sound and the Fury*, it has caused the most furor. With a prescience and boldness unusual for the 1920's O'Neill, in *All God's Chillun Got Wings*, went right to the heart of the racial matter, the sexual relation and miscegenation

Excerpted from *The Plays of Eugene O'Neill* by John Henry Raleigh. Copyright © 1965 by Southern Illinois University Press. Reprinted by permission of the publisher.

and presented a black-white marriage, in which at the end of the play the white actress (Mary Blair) kissed the hand of the Negro actor (Paul Robeson). When these "horrors" were bruited about—the play was published before it was performed—there was a national outcry comparable to that about the Scopes trial although O'Neill's material was much the more incendiary. John S. Sumner of the Society for the Suppression of Vice, said the play should be suppressed; the Mayor of New York received so many complaints about it that he ordered an investigation; there were poison-pen letters, threats from the KKK, and threatened law suits; O'Neill was denounced by the Irish Catholics as a disgrace to their race. Perhaps no play in history received such advance publicity. The company even received a bomb warning. By opening night it had been "legally" established that the white children could not play the opening scene with the colored children (Jimmy Light, one of the Provincetown Players, read that particular scene on the opening night, which was overseen by the police). To O'Neill's disappointment, really, there were no incidents to mar the occasion of the first performance.

Rhythms in *All God's Chillun Got Wings*

As befitting a black-white play, *All God's Chillun Got Wings* is rampant, literally, with the contrasting rhythms of sounds and songs: street noises, popular songs, an organ grinder, and so on. Brooding over the entire play, like the fog horn in *Long Day's Journey*, is a Negro spiritual, sung just before the climactic moment of the play, the marriage of Ella and Jim:

> . . . *a Negro tenor sings in a voice of shadowy richness––the first stanza with a contented, childlike melancholy—*
>
> Sometimes I feel like a mourning dove,
> Sometimes I feel like a mourning dove,
> Sometimes I feel like a mourning dove,
>
> I feel like a mourning dove.
> Feel like a mourning dove.
>
> *The second with a dreamy, boyish exultance––*
>
> Sometimes I feel like an eagle in the air,
> Sometimes I feel like an eagle in the air,
> Sometimes I feel like an eagle in the air,
>
> I feel like an eagle in the air.
> Feel like an eagle in the air.
>
> *The third with a brooding, earthbound sorrow––*

Sometimes I wish that I'd never been born,
Sometimes I wish that I'd never been born,
Sometimes I wish that I'd never been born,

I wish that I'd never been born.
Wish that I'd never been born.

This is the black rhythm; then comes the white rhythm: *"one startling, metallic clang of the church-bell."* At the sound the blacks and whites pour forth and form into two racial lines facing one another, staring at each other with *"bitter hostile eyes."*

RACIAL SEPARATION AS A STATE OF MIND

Some of the points about the racial situation in *All God's Chillun* are fairly obvious; some less so. The obvious one is, of course, that the children, colored and white, who play happily together in Act I, Scene 1, must, as they grow up, diverge into hostile groups. But most of the other characters and situations in the play have some of the irony and subtlety of *Huckleberry Finn* in which two characters, Huck and Jim, have come together as human beings but who have been so profoundly, overwhelmingly stamped with racial categories that these categories have become Kantian configurations in the mind, like the ideas of space and time. By helping Jim, whom he loves, Huck thinks he will go to hell because he helped a "nigger." Jim, on his part, can never think outside of racial terms: "I'd bust him over de head, dat is, if he warn't a white man." As with Twain, the point that O'Neill makes in *All God's Chillun* is that the problem is almost insuperably complex for *any* individual, white or colored, who is involved in it. For the heart of the play resides in the fact that it is not about the economic and legal barriers that impede the rise of the Negro; to the contrary, Jim's father was a successful businessman. Jim is able to go to law school with white students and to take the examinations; he can marry, and in a church at that, a white woman; he can go to live in France with her, to escape. But he can't escape, and has to return, for the play is about inescapable states of mind created by an impossible situation, under which no individual can have the strength and dignity to be himself. Practically all the characters, white or colored, pay some terrible price for a situation they have not personally created.

As *Long Day's Journey into Night* shows degrees of assimilation of the Irish—from the crude peasant Shaughnessy up through the sensitive educated "poet," Edmund Tyrone—so

All God's Chillun shows the degrees of assimilation of the much more deeply set apart and less assimilable Negro. The only well-adjusted Negro character is Jim's mother, and adjusted precisely because she has completely accepted her prescribed role as a "Negro," an "Aunt Jemima," a different order of being from the whites; there is, she says, one road for the whites and another for the blacks. Farther up the scale is the furious Negro whose fury is directed at his fellow Negro who is trying to get ahead in the white man's world and in the white man's way, as Jim is. This is Joe of Act I, Scene 2:

> . . . [*In a rage at the other's* (Jim's) *silence*] You don't talk? Den I takes it out o' yo' hide! [*He grabs* JIM *by the throat with one hand and draws the other fist back*] Tell me befo' I wrecks yo' face in! Is you a nigger or isn't you? [*Shaking him*] Is you a nigger, Nigger? Nigger, is you a nigger?

> JIM. [*looking into his eyes––directly*] Yes. I'm a nigger. We're both niggers. [*They look at each other for a moment.* JOE'S *rage vanishes. . . .*]

But even when one is intelligent and educated, there is still no escape from the psychological malaise. Jim's sister

Hattie is described as a woman of thirty, intelligent, courageous, even powerful, but high-strung and dressed in a severe and mannish manner. She has achieved something, but at the price of chronic nervousness and the loss of her very femininity. And although a schoolteacher, and presumably a good one, she must endure the indignity of the indifferent scorn and sense of superiority of the white ex-prostitute, Ella, whom her brother has married. Thus for Hattie the whites must always be "them." All Negroes, no matter how determined, fall under the mother's somber generalization: "Dey ain't many strong. Dey ain't many happy neider" (II, l).

The only person in the play who almost escapes racial prejudice or hatred is Jim, named, I am sure, for his prototype, the Jim of *Huckleberry Finn*. But again at a terrible price: the inability to sustain himself and his integrity in the presence of whites. He does not have hatred to back him up. He is intelligent, well-educated, unaccented, and hard-working, the equal to any of his white counterparts, but he cannot pass the law examination because (I, 3):

> . . . I swear I know more'n any member of my class. I ought to, I study harder. I work like the devil. It's all in my head— all fine and correct to a T. Then when I'm called on—I stand up—all the white faces looking at me—and I can feel their eyes—I hear my own voice sounding funny, trembling—and all of a sudden it's all gone in my head—there's nothing remembered—and I hear myself stuttering—and give up—sit down— They don't laugh, hardly ever. They're kind. They're good people. [*In a frenzy*] They're considerate, damn them! But I feel branded!

> ELLA. Poor Jim.

> JIM. [*going on painfully*] And it's the same thing in the written exams. For weeks before I study all night. I can't sleep anyway. I learn it all, I see it, I understand it. Then they give me the paper in the exam room. I look it over, I know each answer—perfectly. I take up my pen. On all sides are white men starting to write. They're so sure—even the ones that I know know nothing. But I know it all—but I can't remember any more—it fades—it goes—it's gone. There's a blank in my head—stupidity—I sit like a fool fighting to remember a little bit here, a little bit there—not enough to pass—not enough for anything—when I know it all!

And when the uncomprehending Ella tells him to give it up, he replies: "I need it more than anyone ever needed anything. I need it to live."

THE RACIAL SEPARATION OF ELLA AND JIM

The point that O'Neill is making is that the genuinely intolerable thing about a racial situation is not laws and overt taboos—in the long run these can be overcome—but attitudes; and that the well-meaning white, who still thinks in his heart of hearts that he is a different, and better, being than the Negro, is in some ways harder to bear than the outright racist, who, at least, can be hated. And even Jim himself cannot completely escape the racial habit of mind; thus when in the last scene of the play his by now practically insane wife goads him beyond endurance, it is her very whiteness that is part of her evil, and he calls her a "white devil woman."

The most deeply ingrained racist is the white heroine, Ella Downey. Again the point O'Neill makes with her is acute, especially for the 1920's. Although, as an individual, she loves Jim, her white racial consciousness cannot accept him sexually. Thus she turns sexually inhibited and neurotic and finally almost insane. As with all O'Neill tragic protagonists, her only escape finally is in loss of identity, in her case escape into the past of her childhood when race did not matter. Thus the last scene of the play comes full circle to the first, with Ella once again the innocent little white girl playing with Jim, the innocent little black boy, as in Scene 1. In the words of the last lines of the play:

> ELLA. [*jumping to her feet—excitedly*] Don't cry, Jim! You musn't cry! I've got only a little time left and I want to play. Don't be old Uncle Jim now. Be my little boy Jim. Pretend you're Painty Face and I'm Jim Crow. Come and play!

> JIM. [*still deeply exalted*] Honey, Honey, I'll play right up to the gates of Heaven with you! [*She tugs at one of his hands, laughingly trying to pull him up from his knees as the curtain falls.*]

And behind it all is a primitive sexual-racial fear. Hattie tells Jim that Ella is afraid to have a child by him "because it'll be born black—!" (II, 2).

The point made with Jim is that, because of skin pigmentation, he must be subjected to endless, piled-up humiliations and frustrations. No other character in all of O'Neill's plays, where humiliations and frustrations constitute the web of life, undergoes so many. In Act II, Scene 2, his sister Hattie enumerates for him his sorrows and burdens: that he himself is liable to break down; that his wife, Ella, will be sick a long time; that she, Ella, should go to a sanatorium; that she, the demented Ella, hates, in part anyway, her husband and calls him "Black! Black!"; that she, Hattie, must leave and that Jim, while trying to study for his law examination, must himself now nurse Ella; that Ella will not have a baby by him, her husband; and that Ella should be sent to an asylum or they will probably both go together. After this harrowing series of prophecies Ella herself comes on the stage, carrying a carving knife and calling him, "Nigger." In the last scene of the play, after he announces that he has again failed the law examinations, the happy and triumphant Ella exclaims: "Oh, Jim, I knew it I knew you couldn't! Oh, I'm so glad, Jim! I'm so happy You're still my old Jim—and I'm so glad." It is at this point that he calls her a "white devil."

THE LOSS OF CULTURAL ROOTS

As in *The Emperor Jones*, and in the other racial plays, atavism plays a powerful role, although, as contrasted to *The Emperor Jones*, its role in *All God's Chillun Got Wings* is a positive rather than a negative, the idea being that the African Negro had a culture of his own, worthy of aesthetic comparison to white Western culture and that, when he was torn loose from it, and transplanted to America, he not only lost his genuine cultural roots but was subjected to taking on only the farcical trappings, the parody of his "adopted" culture. Thus in Act II, Scene 1, the apartment of Jim's mother is described: *"On one wall, in a heavy gold frame, is a colored photograph––the portrait of an elderly Negro with an able, shrewd face but dressed in an outlandish lodge regalia, a get-up adorned with medals, sashes, a cocked hat with frills––the whole effect as absurd to contemplate as one of Napoleon's Marshalls in full uniform."* In short, Jim's father gets only a parody of Western culture. But: *"In the left corner, where a window lights it effectively, is a Negro primitive mask from the Congo––a grotesque face, inspiring obscure, dim connotations in one's mind, but beautifully done, conceived in a true religious spirit."* It is this mask, which signifies Negro creativity and sense of beauty, that Ella fears and detests. As the tragedy deepens and as, to suggest this, O'Neill's stage directions have the room shrinking, the mask *"look[s] unnaturally large and domineering"* (II, 2). When Jim announces his failure in the law examinations, Ella grabs the mask from the wall, places it on a table, and plunges a knife through it. The symbolism of the act is fairly obvious, as she explains: "It's all right, Jim! It's dead. The devil's dead. See! It couldn't live—unless you passed. If you'd passed it would have lived in you. Then I'd have had to kill you, Jim, don't you see—or it would have killed me. But now I've killed it (*She pats his hand*). So you needn't ever be afraid any more, Jim" (II, 3).

In O'Neill's deterministic world, the most beset figure is the long-suffering black man, Jim Harris. Joe Mott of *The Iceman Cometh* can escape into alcohol and dreams of glorious yesterdays. Dreamy, of *The Dreamy Kid*, represents the other side of the coin, of which Jim Harris is one side, for he turns, not Christ-like, but fierce and cruel and a killer. Thus at the end of the play, as his dying Mammy (his grandmother) tells Dreamy how he got the name "Dreamy," in the good old days before they came "No'th" to the ghetto which has turned him into a criminal and when Dreamy's boyish eyes were "jest a-dreamin' an' a-dreamin'," the grown-up Dreamy, armed and like a caged tiger, waits for the police to close in on him. But Jim Harris has not even this precarious freedom: "We're never free—except to do what we have to do" (I, 3).

Ironically, it is only back in history, in slavery times, that O'Neill can conceive of the existence of a "free" Negro. This is Cato, the Harford's coachman in *A Touch of the Poet*; as Mrs. Harford describes him: "Cato will be provoked at me for keeping him waiting. I've already caused his beloved horses to be half-devoured by flies. Cato is our black coachman. He also is fond of Simon, although since Simon became emancipated he has embarrassed Cato acutely by shaking his hand whenever they meet. Cato was always a self-possessed free man even when he was a slave. It astonishes him that Simon has to prove that he—I mean Simon—is free" (II).

JIM AND ELLA'S STRUGGLE FOR HAPPINESS

But in the modern megalopolis, no such racial felicity is attainable: to exist with dark skin is to suffer, and to exist with white skin, in proximity to the dark, is to suffer too. O'Neill was sure that *All God's Chillun Got Wings* was one of his "most misunderstood" plays but that someday it would come into its own. What he really meant by its being misunderstood was that in the last analysis, and in its full scope, the play was not a racial play or about the "race problem" but about two human beings and their tragic struggle for happiness; that by the last act Jim and Ella are mankind and its problems. He puts these sentiments into Jim's mouth in Act II, Scene 2: "She's all I've got! You with your fool talk of the black race and the white race! Where does the human race get a chance to come in?" In other words *All God's Chillun* was written in the same spirit as James Baldwin's *Go Tell It on the Mountain,* which, its author claims, is not a "Negro" novel, despite the fact that the principal characters are Negroes. At least one contemporary reader caught O'Neill's ultimate meaning here, and that was T.S. Eliot,[1] who reviewed an O'Neill volume consisting of *All God's Chillun, Desire Under the Elms,* and *Welded* for *The Criterion* in April 1926. Singling out *All God's Chillun* as the most impressive and interesting of the three plays, Eliot said that it had its weaknesses but that O'Neill had got hold of a "strong plot," and had succeeded in giving the problem universality. In "this" respect, said Eliot, O'Neill had been more successful than the author of *Othello,*[2] for O'Neill had finally arrived at the "universal problem of differences which create a mixture of admiration, love, and contempt, with the consequent tension." At the same time O'Neill had never deviated from an exact portrayal of a "possible Negro" and the ending was "magnificent." The other dean of twentieth-century American criticism, Edmund Wilson, was equally enthusiastic about the play—which he saw performed—on its first level, as a racial document, which he called "one of the best things yet written about the race problem of Negro and white and one of the best of O'Neill's plays." With such testimonials as these, it is to be hoped that history itself will someday catch up with the play.

1. American-born English poet   2. tragedy by William Shakespeare

O'Neill's Treatment of Religion

Jerome Ellison

Jerome Ellison explores the role of deity, myth, and religious symbolism in O'Neill's plays. He argues that a central dramatic theme for O'Neill is the relationship between humans and God. Ellison identifies this theme in five of O'Neill's plays, focusing on the most successful, *The Great God Brown.* The two main characters in the play, Dion Anthony and William Brown, represent a duality in the Christian soul that needs to be resolved. Dion is a lover of the worldly life and William is self-denying and focused on life beyond. Ellison contends that in the play Christianity is a force that offers humans a redemptive and ennobling vital truth. Although O'Neill was often puzzled by and angry with God, he never questions the reality of God's universality and power.

Jerome Ellison is an editor, novelist, essayist, and literary critic. He is a professor of English and humanities at the University of New Haven, Connecticut.

Eugene O'Neill, acclaimed almost without a dissenting voice as the ablest playwright America has yet produced, is also the American playwright who was most concerned about man's relations with God. He was wholly conscious of this element in his work and proclaimed it most emphatically as his central theme. "Most modern plays," he said, "are concerned with the relation between man and man, but that does not interest me at all. I am interested only in the relation between man and God." An even more forceful statement appears in a letter of O'Neill's quoted in the "Intimate Notebooks" of George Jean Nathan:

> The playwright today must dig at the roots of the sickness of today as he feels it—the death of the old God and the failure

of science and materialism to give any satisfying new one for the surviving primitive religious instinct to find a meaning for life in, and to comfort its fears of death with. It seems to me that anyone trying to do big work nowadays must have this big subject behind all the little subjects of his plays or novels, or he is simply scribbling around the surface of things and has no more real status than a parlor entertainer. . . .

DEITY IN O'NEILL'S PLAYS

The plays of Eugene O'Neill which most insistently propel onto the stage the problems of relation to Deity are *Anna Christie*, produced in 1921 when O'Neill was thirty-three, *The Great God Brown* (1926), *Lazarus Laughed* (1928), *Dynamo* (1929), and *Days Without End* (1934).

Anna Christie is O'Neill's pristine example of "the big subject behind all the little subjects"—the relation of humans to God as a deep reality behind their relations with each other. The God of *Anna Christie* is a kind of brooding female Poseidon who has usurped the functions of the fates. God, here, is the sea, whom Chris personifies as "dat ole davil," and to whose will all, in the end, submit. "The sea outside—life" was O'Neill's explanation of the symbolism, but Anna invests the sea with godlike purging power, and Mat invests it with benevolence, so it comes on stage as an immanent, living, pagan god.

Lazarus Laughed, besides being O'Neill's purest and most powerful statement of the Christian doctrine that "there is no death," was among the plays of which he was most proud. When asked in 1932 to select the nine of his plays he considered best, he chose *Lazarus Laughed* among them. There were other indications that the playwright ranked *Lazarus*, which he called "the symbolic story of Lazarus' brief second life on earth," with his best work. In 1944 he wrote, "it manages to state a spiritual warning and hope which could be important to-day." When he failed to obtain professional production he exhorted amateurs to try it, saying it was "the kind of thing their theatre should stand for, an American play of the spirit, and a play which should have a message now when death and the meaning or meaninglessness of life are so close to us." However, since the only production was by amateurs at the Pasadena Community Playhouse, *Lazarus* does not qualify as a product of the American commercial theater and therefore, despite its status as America's most eminent playwright's most forthright stage projection of God, must be excluded from the present inquiry.

Dynamo relates the destruction of a young man who loses faith in the "old God of dogma, imagines that he recovers it in the sleek image of an electric dynamo and soon finds himself worshipping it with the same Calvinistic vehemence, superstition and madness. Having violated the vow of chastity made in pious devotion to the new electric god, he casts himself into the dynamo." Kenneth Macgowan said of *Dynamo*: "The dramatist himself wrote that the play is a 'symbolical and factual biography of what is happening in a large section of the American . . . soul right now.'" Nevertheless, *Dynamo* failed to capture the attention of any large section of the American theatergoing public. *Days Without End*, the tale of a distraught modern's return to Catholicism, was pronounced "a failure as an acting play" and lasted only fifty-seven performances of a 1934 Theater Guild production in the Henry Miller Theater. That leaves *The Great God Brown* as the play representing the most successful meeting of O'Neill's heart's desire to clarify man's relation to God and American theatergoers' notions of what they are willing to pay money to see.

THE APPEAL OF *THE GREAT GOD BROWN*

The success at the box office of *The Great God Brown* has always been something of a mystery. The piece was written in Bermuda in 1925 and produced—partly at the playwright's own expense, since Otto Kahn had refused to back it—at the Greenwich Village Theater in 1926. The whole project was felt by its backers to be extremely "iffy." Clark describes some of the talk about it just before the first performance:

> Before the play was put on he [O'Neill] asked what chance I thought it had in the theater, and I said I would give it about two weeks, long enough for the O'Neill fans to take a look at it. "You may be right," he answered, "but I somehow feel there's enough in it to get over to unsophisticated audiences. In one sense *Brown* is a mystery play, only instead of dealing with crooks and police it's about the mystery of personality and life. I shouldn't be surprised if it interested people who won't bother too much over every shade of meaning, but follow it as they follow any story. They needn't understand with their minds, they can just watch and feel."

And O'Neill was right, for the play ran nearly a year.

THE DUALITY OF MAN

In *Brown*, the playwright attempts to explore man's deepest aspirations by following the lives of two men—or, more accurately, man-symbols—Dion Anthony and William Brown, from prep school to middle age, which in Anthony's case is to death. Both men encounter and love two women (or woman-symbols)—Cybele, representing indiscriminate, universal female love and sex for the sake of their own ecstacy, and Margaret, representing love and sex for the sake of reproduction. Masks are used to indicate the differences between the true selves of the characters and the roles they must act for the sake of getting by in society.

THE ROLE OF MASKS

In a 1932 article in the American Spectator *entitled "Memoranda on Masks," O'Neill explains that in certain types of plays the dramatist can effectively use masks to express profound hidden psychological conflicts.*

Not masks for all plays, naturally. Obviously not for plays conceived in purely realistic terms. But masks for certain types of plays, especially for the new modern play, as yet only dimly foreshadowed in a few groping specimens, but which must inevitably be written in the future. For I hold more and more surely to the conviction that the use of masks will be discovered eventually to be the freest solution of the modern dramatist's problem as to how—with the greatest possible dramatic clarity and economy of means—he can express those profound hidden conflicts of the mind which the probings of psychology continue to disclose to us. He must find some method to present this inner drama in his work, or confess himself incapable of portraying one of the most characteristic preoccupations and uniquely significant, spiritual impulses of his time. With his old—and more than a bit senile!—standby of realistic technique, he can do no more than, at best, obscurely hint at it through a realistically disguised surface symbolism, superficial and misleading. But that, while sufficiently beguiling to the sentimentally mystical, is hardly enough. A comprehensive expression is demanded here, a chance for eloquent presentation, a new form of drama projected from a fresh insight into the inner forces motivating the actions and reactions of men and women (a new and truer characterization, in other words), a drama of souls, and the adventures of "Free wills," with the masks that govern them and constitute their fates.

Dion (Dionysus) Anthony (St. Anthony) represents the split, "tortured Christian soul," the creative combination within one person of the gaiety, spontaneity and life-love of the libertine and the self-denying, universal life-love of the dedicated and far-seeing ascetic. Inward tensions and attempts to relieve them through dissipation undermine Dion Anthony's health and finally destroy him. He achieves immortality, however, by bequeathing his mask to William Brown, who represents hardheaded practicality and essentially uncreative worldly success. In the wild, near-hysterical final scene between the dying (dying-god) Dion and Brown, O'Neill rams home a pagan version of the death-and-rebirth theme:

> DION. *(in a steely voice)* I've been the brains! I've been the design! . . . Designing and getting drunk! Saving my woman and children! *(He laughs)* Ha! And this cathedral is my masterpiece! . . . It's one vivid blasphemy from sidewalk to the tips of its spires!—but so concealed that the fools will never know. . . . Well, blasphemy is faith, isn't it? In self-preservation the devil must believe!
>
> . . . . .
>
> Brown loves me! . . . He loves me because I have always possessed the power he needed for love, because I am love!
>
> . . . . .
>
> My last will and testament! I leave Dion Anthony to William Brown. . . . Forgive me, Billy. Bury me
>
> . . . . .
>
> 'Our Father,' . . .
>
> BROWN. *(dully)* He's dead—at last.
>
> . . . . .
>
> BOYS. *(They file out and close the front door as* Brown, *dressed in* Dion's *clothes and wearing his mask, appears at left.)*
>
> MARGARET. *(taking off her mask, gladly)* Dion!
>
> —Act 1, Scene 3

The play is, of course—as was unquestionably O'Neill's intent—capable of a number of interpretations as to the nature of the gods he was placing on, or just behind, his stage. S.K. Winther writes:

> Like most of the leading writers of the modern world, O'Neill is not a Christian in the conventional understanding of Christianity. Rather he is an artist who is concerned with the problem of man's relation to his universe. . . . One way he is sure he will not solve the riddle, and that is the way of traditional Christianity. . . . As popularly conceived, it is an active force for evil, a force that leads man to make dangerous denials, and finally to the inhibition of those qualities that alone make the brief span of this life gleam with occasional moments of real beauty,

a beauty that would come through an admission that we are human and through a vigorous affirmation of our humanity.

This view of O'Neill's striving, though a popular one, leaves out of account certain significant facets of the playwright's struggle as an artist and as a person. There is some evidence that, far from considering Christianity "an active force for evil," O'Neill's true feelings were the exact opposite; he believed Christianity contained some vital truth which, if it could somehow be separated from the corruptions always attendant on human institutions, had redemptive, ennobling power. The progress of the man and his work from *Anna Christie* to *Days Without End* was not such as to carry him farther away from orthodox Christian ideas, but closer to them.

O'Neill seemed endlessly fascinated by the close relationship—denied by Christian hierarchical authorities from the twelfth through the nineteenth centuries—between Christianity and the insights of the more perceptive pagans. Drama critic Helen Muchnic, summing up O'Neill's total effort to get at the significance of any kind of Deistic belief, has this to say: "His plays are eerie with the ghosts of terrible dissatisfactions and of desperate guilt; and their darkness is hardly relieved by a hovering conviction that there is power in love and that an ultimate beneficent grandeur exists beyond the groping and raging consciousness of man."

RELIGIOUS SYMBOLS

Thanks to the ample assistance provided in the playwright's written comments, and from the stage directions in the plays themselves, we have no trouble in locating the historical sources of O'Neill's religious symbols. Dionysus, Cybele, and "dat ole davil" of the sea are all pagan gods of classical antiquity or earlier. Anthony was a Christian saint, Lazarus an important figure of the New Testament. By his treatment of them, O'Neill made it clear that he believed meanings existed in all of them that were important to twentieth-century man—though each individual would have to dig diligently beneath the surface to discover these meanings for himself—and, having discovered them, might find them at variance with popular or institutionalized versions.

THE IMPORTANCE OF MYTH

C.G. Jung, the twentieth-century psychological theorist whose psychology is most hospitable to the Deist hypothesis, never tired of stressing the supreme importance of myth and symbol in human life: "No science," he wrote, "will ever replace myth." O'Neill's whole body of work is an endorsement of this statement; his plays are happy hunting grounds for the kinds of myths, legends, and symbols Jung called "archetypes," "archetypal tales," and "archetypes of the collective unconscious"—patterns of immeasurable antiquity that have been recognized in all historical ages and lands and continue to possess great psychological vitality.

Oscar Cargill has done a study of Jungian forms in O'Neill's work. One of Jung's ideas, it should be noted, is that each individual has an unconscious *anima* (*animus* for females) exhibiting the traits of the sex opposite his own. He regards the rule of opposites—that each conscious trait is matched by an opposing tendency in the unconscious—as universal psychological law. With these preliminaries out of the way, we may now consider Cargill:

> Jung rather than Aeschylus, illuminates *The Great God Brown*. The mask is the face which the Conscious presents to the world—the thing Jung calls the *persona*. It is the direct opposite of a balancing expression in the Unconscious, whence the dualism of O'Neill's characters. For example, the mask of Dion Anthony is "a fixed forcing of his own face—dark, spiritual, poetic . . .—into the expression of a mocking, reckless, . . . sensual young Pan." When Margaret marries Dion . . . it is the *persona* she loves.

> Jung [also] helps in the interpretation of *Lazarus Laughed* (1927), the supreme piece of drama of modern times . . . not only do the young men wear the dress and curled hair of the women, while the young women are attired in the robes of men and wear their hair in a boyish mode, but also there is "the stamp of effeminate corruption" on all the male masks and a "bold masculine expression" on all the female. . . . With utter contempt for the nay-sayers we may pronounce *Lazarus Laughed* as much superior to all other dramatic conceptions in its day as were *Faust, Hamlet,* and *Oedipus Rex* to the contemporary drama of their times.

Returning to our theme, we may conclude with confidence that Eugene O'Neill found God neither dead nor remote. All his life's work time was spent scouting the psychic terrain whence God had been glimpsed and might be glimpsed again. Characters who claim an acquaintance with him frequently appear; the playwright does not ridicule them or discount their testimony. Indeed, God sometimes appears to O'Neill to be most uncomfortably close. His characters sometimes writhe in agony in the presence of his clear will but unable to resolve its contradictions, they beg forgiveness, confess their doubts and sins, hurl their defiance, ask for help. O'Neill may sometimes be angry at God, puzzled by his duality, disappointed in his austerity, but he never ends on a note that seriously questions the reality of some kind of universal, supra-human force or entity of the kind people customarily call God.

Loneliness in *Mourning Becomes Electra*

Winifred L. Dusenbury

In *Mourning Becomes Electra*, Eugene O'Neill creates another lonely, doomed, and isolated family. According to Winifred L. Dusenbury, each member of the Mannon family is damaged by a strict puritanical upbringing. Their Puritan past has conditioned them to hide their emotions and suspect beauty and love as sinful. As a result, the Mannons fail to connect emotionally and are ultimately driven to loneliness and despair. Dusenbury argues that the theme of loneliness is enhanced by O'Neill's effective use of symbolism, particularly the symbols of the island and mask: The island suggests separation and the mask reflects hidden emotions and the inability to communicate.

Winifred Dusenbury is a professor of English at the University of Florida, Gainesville. Her works include (under the name of Winifred Dusenbury Frazer) *Love as Death in "The Iceman Cometh"* and *Emma Goldman and "The Iceman Cometh."* She contributes articles on modern drama to professional journals and magazines.

It is hard to conceive of a family more isolated from society and from each other than the Mannons in Eugene O'Neill's *Mourning Becomes Electra.* One of the chorus of the townspeople in the beginning explains, "They've been top dog around here for near on two hundred years and don't let folks fergit it." It is with trepidation that the townsfolk come close enough to the house to look it over, even though the daughter of the family, Vinnie, has given them permission. A thick wall of fear and jealousy separates the Mannons from all the neighbors. Within the family the hatred for some

Excerpted from *The Theme of Loneliness in Modern American Drama* by Winifred L. Dusenbury (Gainesville: University Press of Florida, 1960). Copyright © 1960 by the Board of Commissioners of State Institutions of Florida. Reprinted by permission of the publisher. (Subheads have been added to the original text by Greenhaven Press. Endnotes in the original have been omitted here.)

members by others and the incestuous love of two couples make each of the four live in lonely misery. Christine, the mother, hates Ezra, the father; the daughter, Lavinia, hates her mother; the son, Orin, hates his father. There is an intense love between mother and son and between father and daughter, which isolates each couple from the other. Lavinia is also in love with her mother's lover, Captain Adam Brant, which gives her two reasons for wishing him dead—that she cannot have him, and that he has disgraced her father. Ezra loves his wife and *she* loves Captain Brant, so that neither Lavinia nor Orin is the undivided recipient of a parent's love which they desire.

Writing on psychiatry in literature, Frederic Wertham says: "The theme of family hates and jealousies is the oldest of plots. Freud would say it is the only one." Adding heavy-handed Freudianism to an ancient dramatic plot, that of Aeschylus' the *Oresteia* trilogy, O'Neill has Americanized the universal emotions of loneliness and sex in an aura of the Puritan conviction of man's guilt.

THE EFFECTS OF PURITANISM

With its vengeful God and its unnatural repression of sensual delights, Puritanism furnishes an ideal motivation for more emphasis than the Greeks gave to loneliness and sublimated sexual instincts. Throughout the three parts of the play there are references to the damaging effects of Puritanism, some made consciously by the characters, some made with unconscious, ironical lack of understanding. But all are made with inferences of the failure of love and the isolation of individuals in an atmosphere of dogmatism. Christine, who has "a fine, voluptuous figure," and who "moves with a flowing animal grace," mocks bitterly at Puritanism in speaking to Lavinia.

> What are you moongazing at? Puritan maidens shouldn't peer too inquisitively into Spring! Isn't beauty an abomination and love a vile thing? (Part One, Act III)

Since her wedding night Christine has suffered a hatred of Ezra for taking her in lust instead of in love. But neither could he be her lover nor let himself be loved, for his belief that "love is a vile thing" is too strong to overcome his normal affectionate feelings. It is her hatred of Ezra and his recognition of it—he says that there has always been "a wall hiding us from each other!"—which motivates the play's action. Feeling isolated from his wife, Ezra has turned to his daughter, Lavinia, for love, and has so entrenched himself in her affections that she says, "I'm not marrying anyone. I've got my duty to Father." Christine has turned to Orin, who was born when his father was away fighting in Mexico. These intense attachments have made any normal family relationships impossible, for they have engendered hate between the mother and daughter and between the father and son.

THE ISOLATION OF EZRA

After Ezra comes back from the Civil War with its horrors still in his mind, he has some inkling of what Christine has long known—that the Calvinistic background of the Mannons has made duty, not love, their ruling passion. He says that all the deaths around him finally made him think of life.

> Before that life had only made me think of death! . . . That's always been the Mannons' way of thinking. They went to the white meeting-house on Sabbaths and meditated on death. Life was a dying. Being born was starting to die. . . . How in hell people ever got such notions. (Part One, Act III)

For the first time in his life Ezra tries to express his love to Christine, but says, "Something queer in me keeps me mum about the things I'd most like to say." With desperate pleading he protests,

> I want to find what that wall is marriage put between us! You've got to help me smash it down! . . . I'm sick of death! I want life! Maybe you could love me now. (Part One, Act III)

Of course Ezra's self-revelation comes too late. Generations attending the white meeting-house have influenced his life too thoroughly for him to be able to remake it. A wall has shut his life from all human beings. As a soldier he has been dubbed Old-stick-in-the-mud, because of his devotion to duty, but he has not been loved. And as he admits, all his affection for Vinnie has been compensation for his failure with Christine: "A daughter's not a wife."

THE ISOLATION OF ORIN

Orin's lack of regard for his father is partly due to jealousy of the attention of the father to his sister, but he too recognizes something of the fatal influence of Puritanism upon Ezra and consequently upon himself. He addresses his father's corpse with mockery.

Death becomes the Mannons! You were always like a statue
of an eminent dead man—. . . Looking over the head of life
without a sign of recognition. . . . You never cared to know me
in life—but I really think we might be friends now you are
dead! (Part Two, Act III)

In the light of Ezra's own words about life and death, Orin's
somewhat facetious remarks about the naturalness of finding
his father dead are appropriate. He recognizes that death will
look familiar upon himself as well. Toward the end of the play,
after he has tried to find life with Lavinia on the South Sea
Islands, where the natives live in a natural state, he admits:

But they turned out to be Vinnie's islands, not mine. They
only made me sick—and the naked women disgusted me. I
guess I'm too much of a Mannon, after all, to turn into a
pagan. (Part Three, Act I, ii)

Pursued by a guilty conscience, Orin finds death his only
recourse and commits suicide. His isolation from the living has
become complete. Only in death can he hope to belong.

THE ISOLATION OF LAVINIA

Lavinia suffers a more remarkable change than does her
father. His experiences during the war, which made him long
for love, not death, are as nothing compared to her experiences
on the Islands.

I loved those Islands. They finished setting me free. There
was something there mysterious and beautiful—a good spirit—of love—coming out of the land and sea. It made me forget death . . . the natives dancing . . . without knowledge of
sin! (Part Three, I, ii)

From a thin, black-dressed, unattractive girl she has become a
voluptuous creature like her mother, who even affects her
mother's colors in dress and who, according to Orin, has stolen
her mother's soul. With almost embarrassing passion she
appeals to Peter to marry her. Her reaction against her
Puritanical upbringing makes her want to break free for eter-
nity. But finally, she too is beaten by the past.

Peter! You trust me with your happiness! But that means
trusting the Mannon dead—and they're not to be trusted with
love! I know them too well! (Part Three, Act IV)

Puritanism wins the day. No belonging to anyone is possible
under its reign. It even isolates those indirectly affected. Peter,
the most kindhearted and gentle of men, becomes alienated
from his mother, his sister, and his town through his relationship to Lavinia.

PETER. I hate this damned town now and everyone in it!
LAVINIA. I never heard you talk that way before, Peter—bitter!
PETER. Some things would make anyone bitter!
LAVINIA. You've quarreled with your mother and Hazel—on account of me. (Part Three, Act IV)

The loneliness which Lavinia must suffer the rest of her days is the logical outcome for a family which has been governed by Puritanical tenets. As Lavinia enters the empty house, never again to leave it, she says with a kind of gloating, "I know they will see to it I live for a long time! It takes the Mannons to punish themselves for being born!" Neither from Puritanism nor from her own loneliness could she escape more than momentarily; then she accepts the retribution of the family background for the rest of her life.

ISLAND SYMBOLISM

Besides the isolation of human beings in an atmosphere in which beauty and love are considered sinful, the theme of loneliness is stressed in *Mourning Becomes Electra* by the use of recurring symbols in many contexts. One of the most important of these is "the island." Suggesting separation from adjoining land and isolation by virtue of the surrounding water, the word is usually used in the play to convey also the idea of escape from a confining environment and from hereditary influences. It also symbolizes paganism in contrast to Puritanism. There, love is not a sin and the God is Pan, not Jehovah. Ironically enough, although the island itself is isolated, it represents a hope of belonging to the world of nature in the minds of those who dream of it. The beauty of the world, which is negated for the Mannons in New England, might become real if they could escape to the island. With despair each one discovers that the island is unattainable and that his loneliness is the more bitter for having dreamed of it. It is, indeed, as in nature, a spot set apart by an insurmountable barrier. . . .

MASK SYMBOLISM

Another symbol of the loneliness of the Mannons is the "mask-like look" which they all wear. The stage directions as each enters reiterate this characteristic. Christine appears to be wearing "a wonderfully life-like pale mask, in which only the deep-set eyes . . . are alive." Lavinia gives the same "strange, life-like mask impression." Of Ezra Mannon,

O'Neill says, "One is immediately struck by the mask-like look of his face in repose." Even Ezra's portrait in the study has the same "semblance of a life-like mask," which his corpse also retains. Orin has the "same life-like mask quality" as his father and Adam Brant. As Christine is about to commit suicide her "face has become a tragic death mask," and after Orin's death, on Lavinia "The Mannon mask-semblance of her face appears intensified now." Even upon the mansion, "The temple portico is like an incongruous white mask fixed on the house to hide its somber gray ugliness." The chorus of townspeople who peer at Christine at the play's opening explain:

> MINNIE. Ayeh. There's somethin' queer lookin' about her face.
> AMES. Secret lookin'—'s if it was a mask she'd put on. That's the Mannon look. They all has it. They grow it on their wives. Seth's growed it on too, didn't you notice—from bein' with 'em all his life. (Part One, Act I)

The refusal or inability of the Mannons to communicate with others has led to their assuming a false face behind which to hide their emotions. Their own feeling of inner isolation has probably been the cause of its assumption. But the mask, once accepted, has also had the effect of making their isolation, not only from outsiders but also from each other, immitigable. The use of the temple portico as a mask upon the Greek-revival mansion of the family indicates a kind of symbolism in the theater which O'Neill well understands. In his article, "Eugene O'Neill as Poet of the Theatre," Alan Downer points out that the playwright in most of his plays enhances the significance of his themes by such symbolism as the appearance of the mansion, which, although realistic, is suggestive also. Its "Puritan gray" walls remind Christine of a tomb, and when Ezra comes home from the war with a new view of life he says, "I can't get used to home yet. It's so lonely." Ezra is of course referring to the feeling which the family as well as the house gives him. O'Neill has made the family and the setting so much a part of each other that the house seems to assume the mask of the Mannon family and the family assumes the coldness of the gray stone, each thus increasing the loneliness of the other. Orin has a realization of this transference of loneliness as he returns.

> Home at last! . . . But the house looks strange. Or is it something in me? . . . Did the house always look so ghostly and dead? (Part Two, Act I)

O'Neill wrote for the stage; his setting enhances his theme. On the symbolic level the cold mansion of Puritanism makes human love impossible except through escape to a pagan South Seas island, half a world away.

The purpose, action, and form of *Mourning Becomes Electra* all conduce to the effect of a unified drama. The purpose of the play—to show the disastrous effect of man's attempt to repress his sensuous nature—is well served by the action, which consists of one incident after another portraying the alienation of Ezra from Christine, of Orin from his father, of Lavinia from her mother, and then of Lavinia from her father, of Christine from her lover, of Orin from his mother, and finally of Orin from Lavinia and of Lavinia from Peter. The form controls the action with climactic separations through death at the conclusion of each of the three Parts. At the end of "Homecoming" Lavinia cries to her dead father, "Don't leave me alone. Come back to me!" At the end of "The Hunted," Orin grieves frantically for his mother. "I've got to find her! I've got to make her forgive me. . . . But she's dead—She's gone." At the end of "The Haunted" Orin kills himself and Lavinia enters the house to live "alone with the dead." Each death brings retributive action which results in another death, until Lavinia is left alone to suffer for them all.

O'Neill's Harmonious Vision in *Ah, Wilderness!*

Edwin A. Engel

According to Edwin A. Engel, *Ah, Wilderness!* is unlike O'Neill's other plays because it is the only one that positively depicts a middle-class family. The Millers' positive home life is diametrically opposed to O'Neill's personal family experience, Engel argues; thus *Ah, Wilderness!* is O'Neill "wishing out loud."

Unlike the families in his other plays, the Millers are headed by a loving and sympathetic father. Nat Miller, who is tolerant, humorous, and tender, does not personify the hidden motives, neuroses, obsessions, fixations, and interpersonal difficulties that haunt the other O'Neill father figures. Likewise, Mrs. Miller is unlike other O'Neill mothers and wives. She is soft and maternal rather than stubborn, distraught, or nervous. Engel interprets Richard, the son, to be a comic counterpart of the troubled, agonizing adolescents found in O'Neill's other dramas. Untouched by evil impulses and corrupting influences, Richard faces a future that is secure and happy. Engel argues that the theme of *Ah, Wilderness!* is the passage from the creative and exploratory period of youth to a more seasoned stage of maturation supported by love and peace.

Edwin A. Engel taught at the University of Michigan. He is a contributor to *Ideas in the Drama: Selected Papers from the English Institute* as well as various professional journals.

O'Neill is said to have awakened one morning "with the story, characters, plot scheme and practically all the details of *Ah, Wilderness!* in his mind clamoring to be put down on paper." Having enjoyed his beatific wish-fulfillment dream,

Reprinted by permission of the publisher from *The Haunted Heroes of Eugene O'Neill* by Edwin A. Engel (Cambridge, MA: Harvard University Press). Copyright © 1953 by the President and Fellows of Harvard College.

he converted it into a play within a month. Still under the influence of the dream he declared that his

> purpose was to write a play true to the spirit of the American large small-town at the turn of the century. Its quality depended upon atmosphere, sentiment, an exact evocation of the mood of a dead past. To me the America which was (and is) the real America found its unique expression in such middle-class families as the Millers among whom so many of my own generation passed from adolescence into manhood.

Fully awake, he described *Ah, Wilderness!* not only as "a comedy of recollection," but as "a dream walking." At no other time in his playwriting career did O'Neill respond to the pleasant, harmonious simplicity of the "real America" or regard "such middle-class families as the Millers" with anything more affectionate than disdain. Indeed, it is unlikely that reality had ever before seemed so agreeable to him. For even as a young man, a cub reporter, he displayed the quality of mind that manifested itself in the tragedies that he was to write, a mind that was unable "to dwell on a group of happily placed characters . . . without reaching out further and discovering the inevitable underlying submerged group that . . . contributed to the happy placement." Himself a member of the submerged group prior to his newspaper days, a vagrant and an inebriate, he must have viewed the world during that time through jaundiced eyes. Nor were his first marriage, which he called a mistake, or the situation which led him to attempt suicide, conducive to any but a tragic apprehension of reality. And if O'Neill's adolescence, which coincided with that of the hero of *Ah, Wilderness!*, was not so wretched as his early manhood, it was still not a time when he could have felt that "life *was* love." The only permanent home that O'Neill had known was the family summer place in New London. Throughout most of the year he was away at prep school, his father on the road. As for middle-class stability, one would not expect to find it in the family of an actor. For a more accurate family portrait one should probably turn to *The Great God Brown* wherein the young Dion Anthony, deprived of love and protection, approached maturity in spite and bitterness. Years later, referring to *Ah, Wilderness!* O'Neill confirmed the wish-fulfillment character of the play. "That's the way I would have liked my boyhood to have been," he said. "It was a sort of wishing out loud." Although O'Neill's dream reflected and contributed to his temporary calm repose, it was Apollonian only in the blandest sense. Revealing his innermost being at a time when it was never less turbulent, the dream arrived at a truth that was about as high as that achieved by a Norman Rockwell cover for *The Saturday Evening Post.*

THE POSITIVE MOOD OF THE PLAY

If *Ah, Wilderness!* disregards the religious aspect of *Days Without End,* it compensates by sharing the moral attitude expressed in that play. Precisely as John Loving's interlude of foolish radicalism, atheism, and paganism was treated with gentle ridicule and forgiving censoriousness by Father Baird, similar experiments of Richard Miller are regarded with mingled mirth and mild concern by the loving father of the family in *Ah, Wilderness!* Having renounced in *Days Without End* his own follies of the preceding couple of decades, O'Neill now looked upon them as amusing aberrations of a sensitive, earnest adolescent. If the hero were born with ghosts in his eyes, they have long since been exorcised, and with them the "spirit of evil." Freed of rationalistic skepticism, O'Neill was not inclined to burden Richard with ambiguities and masks. Liberated from incertitude, he was driven neither to mocking irony nor to pathos and "black despair." In *Ah, Wilderness!* there is no problem of existence; no fighting of life or fear of death; no probing of hidden motives; no unfulfilled longings, neuroses, or obsessions; no father-son hostility, mother fixation, or marital difficulty. Here, without its piety, is John Loving's blissful youth, secure and happy in the bosom of the family.

Even the stage directions reflect O'Neill's currently cheerful mood. Thus, the *sitting room of the Miller home in a large small-town in Connecticut*—New London, presumably—is *homely looking and cheerful in the morning sunlight, furnished with scrupulous medium-priced tastelessness of the period.* In the bookcases are *books the family really have read. A medium-priced inoffensive rug covers most of the floor. The walls are papered with a cheerful, ugly blue design.* One is reminded of the sitting-room of another middle-class home, one which O'Neill described when he was in a less expansive state of mind. Having indicated that Mrs. Dion Anthony's house was located in *one of those one-design districts that daze the eye with multiplied ugliness,* O'Neill explained that the *background is a backdrop on which the rear wall is painted with the intolerable lifeless realistic detail of the stereotyped paintings which usually adorn the sitting rooms of such houses.*

CHARACTERIZATION OF THE PARENTS

Tolerant in *Ah, Wilderness!* of bourgeois tastelessness and ugliness, he was more than forbearing with the perpetrators of such offenses. Even the father—indeed, *especially* the father—is treated with uncommon affection. If Richard is the hero, he divides the role with Nat Miller, as did Eben Cabot with Ephraim.[1] Nat, to be sure, resembles Ephraim not at all. For, like the late Mr. Loving,[2] he is "a fine man" and the antithesis of all the other fathers in O'Neill's plays. Nat

> is in his late fifties, a tall, dark, spare man, a little stoop-shouldered, more than a little bald, dressed with an awkward attempt at sober respectability imposed upon an innate heedlessness of clothes. His long face has large, irregular, undistinguished features, but he has fine, shrewd, humorous gray eyes.

Shrewd and humorous, he is also tolerant, relaxed, tender, loving. The *pater familias*, he is also Mrs. Miller's little boy. Mrs. Miller is a "perfect type of our old beautiful ideal of wife and mother" and the exact counterpart of no other O'Neill mother. She

> is around fifty, a short, stout woman with fading light-brown hair sprinkled with gray, who must have been decidedly pretty as a girl in a round-faced, cute, small-featured, wide-eyed fashion. She has big brown eyes, soft and maternal—a bustling, mother-of-a-family manner.

Her maternity is not possessive, not even obtrusive. Since her husband is no ogre, she is not, like Dion's mother,[3] thin, frail, faded, nervous, distraught; or, like Mrs. Light,[4] stubborn and rebellious. Nor is she bovine and dreamy like Mrs. Fife,[5] for there is nothing of the Earth Mother in her. If anything, Mrs. Miller is the type of middle-class mother, the Mother's Day Mother.

CHARACTERIZATION OF RICHARD MILLER

It is not surprising that the off-spring of this harmonious pair—of the fine father and the ideal mother—should be a son who reflects their harmony, their perfection of character. Richard Miller

> is going on seventeen, just out of high school. In appearance he is a perfect blend of father and mother, so much so that each is convinced he is the image of the other. He has his mother's

---

1. in *Desire Under the Elms*   2. in *Days Without End*   3. in *The Great God Brown*
4. in *Dynamo*   5. in *Dynamo*

light-brown hair, his father's gray eyes; his features are neither
large nor small; he is of medium height, neither fat nor thin.
One would not call him a handsome boy; neither is he home-
ly. But he is definitely different from both of his parents,
too. . . . There is something of extreme sensitiveness added—a
restless, apprehensive, defiant, shy, dreamy, self-conscious intel-
ligence about him. In manner he is alternately a plain simple
boy and a posey actor playing a role.

Although his personality is potential for tragedy, Richard is
the comic counterpart of such characters as Jim Harris,
Dion Anthony, Charlie Marsden, Reuben Light, John
Loving—all of whom had passed through painful adolescence into the agonies of adulthood. His prototype is the
young Marco Polo.[6] Whereas Marco, increasingly dominated
by his acquisitive instinct, twisted by the influence of his
father and of his uncle, passed into vicious manhood,
Richard, living in the "real America" of 1906, a member of
the middle-class Miller family, remains untouched by evil
impulses, free of corruptive influences. For *Ah, Wilderness!*
is indeed a blissful dream in which characters out of the
tragic reality of the other plays make their appearance
divested of all their former significance: Thus Sid Davis is a
drunk, but he is described as *short and fat, bald-headed,*
with the Puckish face of a Peck's Bad Boy who has never
grown up. In his drunken state, far from stupefied, he radi-
ates happiness. Indolent, and at odds with his middle-class
family, he is happily tolerated by them. Muriel's father, the
cause of Richard's innocent orgy, is the counterpart of the
dark fathers of the tragedies. But the part he plays is a slight
one; his baleful presence cannot dim the bright atmosphere
of the play. The prostitute, for the first time since *Anna*
Christie, has no symbolic significance, no permanent effect
upon the character or destiny of the hero. Far from being
haunted by his memory of the tart, Richard boastfully confesses the incident to Muriel the following evening. Like
Marsden's,[7] his is a fugitive virtue; but he is not given, as was
dear old Charlie, to guilty introspection about sinful acts
unconsummated. In *Ah, Wilderness!* O'Neill does not follow
his usual practice of completing the life cycle of his hero. Yet
he assures us that Richard's future will be secure and happy.
At the end of the play Nat Miller says of him: "And I don't
think we'll ever have to worry about his being safe—from

6. in *Marco Millions*   7. in *Strange Interlude*

himself—again. And I guess no matter what life will do to him, he can take care of it now." Indeed, the boy may look forward to the enjoyment of that state of harmony, fulfillment, and contentment which the parents experience at the final curtain when, standing in the moonlight with his arm around his wife, Nat recites from the *Rubaiyat* with a *gentle nostalgic memory*:

'Yet Ah, that Spring should vanish with the Rose!

That Youth's sweet-scented manuscript should close!'

Then throwing off his melancholy he says *with a loving smile,* "Well, Spring isn't everything, is it, Essie? There's a lot to be said for Autumn. That's got beauty, too. And Winter— if you're together." With Essie beside him singing in the Wilderness, Nat finds that Wilderness is Paradise enow. Death being dead, life laughs with love. Nat appears to be enjoying the benefits of that revelation. Less fortunate than he, the tragic heroes have had to face the terrors of the wilderness alone, lost without love, shrinking fearfully from both life and death. Perplexed by both the problems of existence and of non-existence, some sought comfort in the concept of the renewal of life, in the pagan Earth Mother's annunciation that "spring comes again bearing life! Always again!" Craving love and peace, others returned to childhood or to the source of life and love, the Mother. But Nat Miller has no need of either myth or psychology. Wistful at first about the passing of Spring, he quietly renounces its glories, proclaims the beauty of Autumn, anticipates without displeasure the approach of Winter—provided that his wife be with him.

THE PLAY'S MAJOR THEME

Although Spring is pleasant, it "isn't everything." This, the theme of *Ah, Wilderness!* is developed by juxtaposing Spring and Autumn, adolescence and maturity, son and father. Formerly the season of Dionysian intoxication, of the eruption of the creative life force, Spring and Youth in other O'Neill plays have never passed without regret. Now, Autumn is Spring improved with age, and Nat is the callow Richard nourished by long years of peace and love. Attractive though it is, Spring is the time of minor hazards: of harmless impulses, naive notions, innocuous indiscretions. Richard, as his father explains, is only a fool kid who's just at the stage when he's out to rebel against all authority, and so he grabs at everything radical to read and wants to pass it on to his elders and his girl and boy friends to show off what a young hellion he is!

The father, having passed through a similar period, understands the son. Urged by Mrs. Miller to give Richard "a good talking to" about "those awful books" he is reading, Nat says *with a grin,* "I know there's nothing to it anyway. When I think of the books I used to sneak off and read when I was a kid." With Richard upon the carpet, Nat's demeanor is one of ill-concealed delight. There is *a twinkle* in his eye when the son, *frowning portentously,* declares, "I don't believe in this silly celebrating the Fourth of July—all this lying talk about liberty—when there is no liberty!" He puts his *hand to his mouth to conceal a grin* when Richard, *getting warmed up,* adds:

> The land of the free and the home of the brave! Home of the slave is what they ought to call it—the wage slave ground under the heel of the capitalist class, starving, crying for bread for his children, and all he gets is a stone! The Fourth of July is a stupid farce!

And, he is *greatly amused* when Richard *adds grimly,* "No, you can celebrate your Fourth of July. I'll celebrate the day the people bring out the guillotine again and I see Pierpont Morgan being driven by in a tumbril!" An "advanced thinker"—like John Loving—Richard has been reading the pagan poetry of . . . Omar Khayyam. "'The Rubaiyat . . .' That's the best of all!" In 1906 everybody is reading *the Rubaiyat,* Nat Miller explains to his scandalized wife, "and it don't seem to do them any harm. There's fine things in it, it seems to me—true things," a judgment which, as we have seen, he bears out as the play ends. Indeed, the Rubaiyat was being read as late as 1919 when, in *The Straw,* O'Neill had his hero parody one of its verses:

> 'A glass of milk, and thou
> Coughing beside me in the wilderness—
> Ah—wilderness were Paradise enow!'

Nat continues to be amused even with the sexual aspects of his son's advanced thought. He defends Richard against McComber's angry charge that the boy is "dissolute and blasphemous" and is trying "to corrupt the morals" of his young daughter, Muriel. But then as Nat reads Richard's transcriptions of voluptuous love poems by Swinburne, the *irrepressible boyish grin* leaves his face. With *a trace of shocked reproof showing in his voice* he says to his brother-in-law, Sid,

> But it's no joking matter. That stuff *is* warm, if you ask me! I don't like this a damned bit, Sid. That's no kind of thing to be sending a decent girl. *(More worriedly)* I thought he was really stuck on her—as one gets stuck on a decent girl at his age—all moonshine and holding hands and a kiss now and again. But this looks—I wonder if he is hanging around her to see what he can get? *(Angrily)* By God, if that's true, he deserves that licking McComber says it's my duty to give him! I've got to draw the line somewhere!

Whereupon he asks Richard whether he has "been trying to have something to do with Muriel—something you shouldn't—you know what I mean." Richard *stares at him for a moment as if he couldn't comprehend—then, as he does, a look of shocked indignation comes over his face.* "No!" he exclaims. "What do you think I am, Pa? I never would! She's not that kind! Why, I—I love her! I'm going to marry her— after I get out of college! She's said she would! We're engaged!" *With great relief* the father says, "All right. That's all I wanted to know. We won't talk any more about it." Vindicated, the son, we may be sure, will follow in his father's footsteps. If the Awakening of Spring has been marked by an impulse to rebel against all authority, it remains, in the case of Richard Miller, singularly free of all other irresistible, fateful forces. Although for a seventeen-year-old Richard is precocious in certain respects, his sexual development is obviously arrested. But the rewards of sexual anesthesia, of purity, are apparent. They are those which Nat is now enjoying. And they exist only in the sentimental pipe-dream.

The Tragic Vision in *The Iceman Cometh*

Horst Frenz

Horst Frenz argues that the characters in O'Neill's *The Iceman Cometh* are too frail to confront reality. He states that they cannot face the truth about themselves: their capacity for evil, their fears, and their insecurities. As a result, they cling to illusions. Frenz writes that *The Iceman Cometh* is not a tragedy in the Greek sense in which characters suffer the consequences of a tragic flaw. Rather, O'Neill's tragedy grows from the psychological ordeal that the characters experience when they are stripped of their illusions.

Horst Frenz is a professor of English at Indiana University and a consultant for the National Endowment for the Arts. The editor of *Nobel Lectures: Literature, 1901–1967* and *American Playwrights on Drama*, he has published many articles about American and European drama.

In *The Iceman Cometh*, O'Neill reverted once more to the past, to his New York days at Jimmy the Priest's. The action takes place in a shabby saloon somewhere in midtown New York in the year 1912. In this gloomy atmosphere, O'Neill assembles a group of seedy characters most of whom have given up any occupation they ever had and abandoned themselves to drink and their wishful illusions. Like Ibsen, especially in his *The Wild Duck*, O'Neill presents the human condition as such that man cannot live without clinging to some illusion or "life-lie." About a dozen of his characters are sprawled out on the iron chairs or asleep with their heads on the grimy tables. From time to time they ask the proprietor, an equally sorry character named Harry Hope, to stand them a drink. They are all waiting for Hickey, a hardware salesman who drops in once

Excerpted from *Eugene O'Neill* by Horst Frenz. Copyright © 1971 by Frederick Ungar Publishing Co., Inc. Reprinted with the permission of The Continuum Publishing Group.

a year to celebrate Harry's birthday. But the Hickey who shows up this time is not the familiar old joker who regales them with lusty stories of his wife and the iceman. He is as friendly as ever, but he is sober, and he has come with a purpose: to get them to see the light, to free themselves from their illusions. He has found happiness himself and wants the others to share it. But this happiness stems from the loss of his last illusion: he has realized that tomorrow holds no promise for him, and this is why he is at peace.

With his slick sales talk Hickey shakes his friends out of their twilight existence, provokes them, shocks them with his accusations that they are too cowardly to face the truth, and bewilders them with his promise of peace and contentment. Harry Hope and his pals resolve to look life in the face. One after another they go off to seek jobs. Hickey knows that they will not succeed, and he is right: the peace he has promised them is not forthcoming. Yet they still fail to realize that their only future is death. Their illusions return; they recover their taste for whiskey. Only the young anarchist who cannot forgive himself for betraying his mother takes the ultimate step and throws himself out of the window. Finally it comes out that Hickey has murdered his wife to put an end to the suffering he has caused her. His "call" to liberate the others from their illusions about life is seen to be a cloak to protect his own greater and more tragic illusion. The arrival of Hickey, the "iceman" or death, means the end of illusion, and hence the end of life.

O'NEILL COMPARED WITH GORKI

Much in *The Iceman Cometh* derives from O'Neill's own experiences at Jimmy the Priest's dive on the New York waterfront, where a friend of his once committed suicide. Its similarity to Maksim Gorki's *The Lower Depths* is probably not coincidental, for O'Neill once said of this play that it "is really more wonderful propaganda for the submerged than any other play ever written, simply because it contains no propaganda, but rather shows humanity as it is—truth, in terms of human life." Yet the two plays present this truth in different ways.

Despite their similarities—in setting, character types, themes (escape from reality, the necessity of illusion), emphasis on dialogue rather than on action, situation (symbolic of the human condition), treatment of the central figure as catalyst—there remain important differences between the two plays: Gorki's play is socially oriented, designed to motivate social action, whereas O'Neill's play is psychologically oriented, designed to reveal the weakness or evil in man. *The Lower Depths* revolves around ethical problems of man in society, while *The Iceman Cometh* deals with the innate nature of the individual, the existential problems of the individual's flight from reality into the realm of illusion.

O'Neill's characters are not social outsiders proudly and deliberately avenging themselves on a social system they hate, but rather victims of their inherently human vulnerability to life-lies. This four-act play again combines symbolic and realistic elements. The language is realistic, sometimes brutal. The characterization is superb. Unlike most of O'Neill's other plays, *The Iceman Cometh* is not very experimental, unless the Ibsen-like tendency of concealing the motives of a central character until the end of the play can be called an experiment. In O'Neill's case, this delayed exposition requires that the audience, in spite of the extraordinary length of the play, reinterpret Hickey's words and actions in the light of the final disclosure.

THE ICEMAN COMETH AS TRAGEDY

In *The Iceman Cometh*, O'Neill rejected the pseudo-Greek classicism of *Mourning Becomes Electra*. At the heart of his play, there is neither the conflict between divine will and human happiness, nor the tragic flaw of the dramatic hero, but rather the paradox of the human condition in which dream is reality and reality dream, in which despair becomes hope and hope despair. Man is too frail to withstand the stark truth of reality and must, in order to survive, renounce it in favor of self-delusion. As Larry Slade, one of Harry Hope's roomers, says:

> To hell with the truth! As the history of the world proves, the truth has no bearing on anything. It's irrelevant and immaterial, as the lawyers say. The lie of a pipe dream is what gives life to the whole misbegotten mad lot of us, drunk or sober.

The element of tragedy, if it can be so called, arises here not from a tragic flaw in the classical Greek sense, but from the denial of one's illusion or pipe dreams. Indebted, perhaps, to Schopenhauer or Freud, O'Neill depicts the fundamental paradox of self-fulfillment through annihilation. Hickey's guilt is not motivated by revenge against an unfaithful wife. On the contrary, his wife has been too faithful and too devoted.

"That's what made it so hard," admits Hickey, "That's what made me feel such a rotten skunk—her always forgiving me." Hickey's criminal act is the result not of hatred or vengeance, but of his own inability to return the love his wife had given him for so long. It is the recognition of this weakness or inadequacy, his self-admission of the truth about himself, that brings about his crime.

THE PLAY'S PESSIMISM

Hickey seeks peace of mind in the destruction of his last illusion, the illusion of his wife's infidelity with the iceman. But the end of illusion signals the end of life: "Do you suppose I give a damn about life now?" Hickey exclaims to the detective, "Why you bonehead, I haven't got a single damned lying hope or pipe dream left!" In reality, there has been no iceman for his wife. Hickey himself has become the "iceman"—death, the destroyer of life-sustaining illusion.

Although *The Iceman Cometh* is perhaps too deliberately eschatological, too determined to avoid the superficial, O'Neill at least attempts to confront fundamental problems of human existence, to present in dramatic terms a tragic vision of life. In an article in *Life* of 2 December 1946, it was suggested that two conclusions can be drawn from this play: that great tragedy contradicts the spirit of American democracy, and that it is incompatible with the American belief in progress. This raises the question whether tragic greatness is possible in America, whether consciousness of evil, fear, and insecurity can be meaningfully treated, and whether such a meaningful artistic treatment can help man attain new dignity. *The Iceman Cometh* gives a negative answer, but *Long Day's Journey into Night* will show that this dignity is not unattainable—even in America.

CHAPTER 4

Two Late Autobiographical Plays

The Illusion of Home in O'Neill's Plays

Jay L. Halio

Jay Halio writes that Eugene O'Neill's plays portray the human quest to find a home or a place where one belongs. In O'Neill's early works, including his first produced play *Bound East for Cardiff*, the main characters dream of happiness that comes with a stable marriage, family, home, and a connection with others. But this dream, according to Halio, is only an illusion that is inevitably wrecked by the unhappy experiences of life.

The home as an illusion is a theme found throughout O'Neill's work; its most vivid portrayal is in his greatest play, *Long Day's Journey into Night*. The members of the Tyrone family discover that their dream of happiness as a family is a baseless illusion destroyed by drugs, guilt, fear, and illness. Even brief glimpses of peace that Edmund experienced at sea only emphasize the torment he experiences at home. Halio draws the conclusion that for O'Neill the home represents a search for love, happiness, and acceptance that is sadly unfulfilled.

Jay Halio is an English professor at the University of Delaware, Newark. He is the editor of *Shakespeare, Man of the Theater* and *Dictionary of Literary Biography, Volume XIV: British Novelists Since 1960*. He is also a contributor to *Southern Review* and *Shakespeare Quarterly*.

In the first O'Neill play ever produced, "Bound East for Cardiff," a dying seaman complains to his friend:

> YANK. This sailor life ain't much to cry about leavin'—just one ship after another, hard work, small pay, and bum grub; and when we get into port, just a drunk endin' up in a fight, and all your money gone, and then ship away again. Never meetin'

Excerpted from "Eugene O'Neill: The Long Quest" by Jay L. Halio, in *Modern American Drama: Essays in Criticism*, edited by William E. Taylor (DeLand, FL: Everett/Edwards, 1968). Reprinted by permission of the author.

no nice people; never gittin' outa sailortown, hardly, in any port; travelin' all over the world and never seein' none of it; without no one to care whether you're alive or dead. . . . There ain't much in all that that'd make yuh sory to lose it, Drisc.

DRISCOLL. *(gloomily)* It's a hell av a life, the sea.

YANK. *(musingly)* It must be great to stay on dry land all your life and have a farm with a house of your own with cows and pigs and chickens, 'way in the middle of the land where yuh'd never smell the sea or see a ship. It must be great to have a wife, and kids to play with at night after supper when your work was done. It must be great to have a home of your own, Drisc.

Yank's vision of "a home of your own" was never to be fulfilled, neither for Yank nor for most of the characters in O'Neill's long and fruitful dramatic career launched that night in Provincetown in 1916. But the quest remained central to O'Neill's work, and the earnestness of this seeking as much as his indefatigable experimentation with technique greatly contributed to the revitalization of the American theater in the early decades of his century—even as one illusion of "home" after another was examined and found for what it was—an illusion.

THE ILLUSION OF HOME IN THE EARLY PLAYS

In "The Long Voyage Home," the next play in the series *S.S. Glencairn,* the Swede Olson seems about to realize Yank's dream of settling down on a farm after years at sea. He has two years' pay saved to buy a farm, after he returns to his mother and brother in Stockholm. But although when he hits port he resolutely keeps off the drink that has wrecked all his previous dreams of returning home, Olson is yet a prey to the treachery of men like Fat Joe and the whore, Freda, who drug him, rob him, and then shanghai him aboard the notorious ship "Amindra." So poor Olson never makes it home. But what if he had? The answer lies in another play of the sea, really a kind of sequel to "The Long Voyage Home," if also a full-length play in its own right. Chris Christopherson, in *Anna Christie*, voices many of the same sentiments as Yank or Olson about a sailor's life and "dat ole davil, sea." Like Olson he has followed the sea, never—or seldom—getting back home, until his wife tires of waiting for him and leaves Sweden for relatives in Minnesota. When she dies, Chris decides to let their little daughter remain on the farm with her cousins so that she will never know a father like him or the life of the sea. But Chris's notion of a happy, healthy life on the farm is cruelly wrong: Anna's real history up to her arrival in New York to find him years later makes this point clear. Her cousins, hardly benevolent, have worked her to the marrow, seduced her, and generally treated her more like an animal than a human being, let alone kin. Ironically, it is at sea, aboard her father's barge, that Anna begins to find the peace of mind and harmony of spirit that restores her health and well-being. It is also at sea aboard the barge that she meets the shipwrecked sailor, Mat Burke, who comes out of the fog one night and recognizes the real strength and beauty that now stand revealed in her.

When Mat and Anna fall in love, Chris opposes their union: he wants something better for his daughter than anything that "dat ole davil sea" has spewed up for her. He fails to understand the changes in Anna, and what Mat can mean to her, partly because he is ignorant of her past and partly because he is deeply prejudiced: he knows too well what being married to a sailor would be like. On her part, Anna loves Mat too much to marry him, being what she has been. It is not until she tells both Mat and Chris the truth about herself that any real union is possible, or that any reconciliation between the two men can occur.

But though the play seems to end happily, its last words strike again a note of gloom and foreboding, as Chris mutters: "Fog, fog, fog, all bloody time. You can't see vhere you vas going, no. Only dat ole davil, sea—she knows!" In this, and in the play's strong undercurrent of morbid fatalism, there is much to support O'Neill's own view that the ending is not really happy, that in it we can find little cause for genuine rejoicing over these poor souls, whose pasts will inevitably rise up to wreck their meager chances for happiness. Boy-gets-girl was not necessarily a happy outcome in O'Neill's opinion or in his experience, as another early play, *Beyond the Horizon*, bitterly demonstrates. The promise of a loving marriage may too often turn out to be just another illusion. Sacrificing his vision of freedom, of life over the rim of the hills that have imprisoned his spirit, Robert Mayo does so for the love of a girl who, he later discovers, cannot begin to match his dreams. Still, as the later—and greater—plays show, if there is any hope for man at all, if there is any "home" for him this side of the tomb, it is in the love of a generous-hearted woman, or someone who can help him find a faith in and beyond himself by which he may live. The quest for home thus becomes a quest for love and for conviction, but in O'Neill's work it is a quest that more often than not remains tragically unfulfilled.

THE ILLUSION OF HOME IN *LONG DAY'S JOURNEY INTO NIGHT*

Long Day's Journey into Night is not only, by common consent, the greatest of O'Neill's plays (and, ironically, one he never saw—or wished to see—produced in his lifetime); it is also the drama which most powerfully and autobiographically examines those forces which impel many of his other works. It is thus the central document of his dramatic career. Concerned with members of a single family, it explores within the compass of a single, critical day the pressures—and the causes of those pressures—which, despite the love each one feels for the others, compel them to drive one another to despair. The action takes place in August, 1912, at the summer home of the Tyrones. James Tyrone, a famous American actor (modeled on O'Neill's father, James O'Neill), has earned a fortune since the days when, as an Irish immigrant kid, he had to work in sweatshops to help support his mother and brothers and sisters. He has spent most of this money, however, on bad real estate investments, and the only thing he has to show for them is this summer home which, his wife Mary complains, is not a home at all. Most of the year they are on the road with the play that has made him famous but for which he has sacrificed what might otherwise have been a distinguished career as a Shakespearean actor. His Irish origins, his profession, the notoriety of his sons' behavior, and other causes have also combined to exclude the family from the genteel society that his wife knew before marriage and longs to return to, with ever diminishing hopes.

For Mary has never been able to fit in with her husband's professional friends, nor—unhappy and lonely though she remains—has she been able to break with the man she knows loves her and whom she also loves, despite his failure to provide the home that she so desperately wants and needs. This is her predicament, and it is seriously complicated by her feelings of guilt over the death of her infant son, Eugene, and the present illness of her youngest son, Edmund. Unable to find other solace, she relapses into the drug addiction that began with Edmund's painful birth and has helped ever since to shut her off from present painful realities.

As the play opens, it is a sunny, summer morning in what seems to be an ordinary family home. But it is not long before signs of mounting tension appear. For the last two months—or since her most recent return from a sanitorium—Mary has apparently been well enough to give her family the sense of "home" that they have also missed and that her sons Jamie and Edmund have come to regard as a priceless gift. But Edmund's wretched health, the fear that he may have consumption—the cause of her father's death— have already begun to revive feelings that she has hitherto found unbearable. Her wandering around sleeplessly the previous night, her growing nervousness, the beginnings of her withdrawal from normal relationships increasingly worry her husband and her sons, who now see (and not without feelings of guilt themselves) their hopes for a continuing, stable home badly threatened. As Mary resumes her drug-taking, their worst fears are realized, and they feel cruelly cheated by what they are now forced to consider a baseless illusion, a dream of happiness as hopeless as any of those of the past which make Mary their victim by the end of the play.

Mary's lapsing into drug addiction affects her family in other ways besides their sense of betrayal and deprivation. For James, her leaving them in this way brings doubts about the meaning of his own life and reduces him, finally, to a doubly defeated and broken old man. Trying to justify his mistakes—his surrender of nobler aspirations, his real estate ventures, his stinginess—he wonders now what it was he wanted to buy that could have been worth such sacrifice, and he can find no answer. For Jamie, the older son, his mother's breakdown causes him to break down also. Had she been able to keep off drugs, he feels he could have kept off his poison—the drinking, whoring, and bitter cynicism that now return to claim him. Edmund's situation is at once more desperate and more hopeful. Afflicted definitely by consumption, and worried that his father, superstitiously believing the disease is fatal, may send him to a cheap state hospital, Edmund is further tormented by the thought that his mother has forsaken him, too. But unlike Jamie, he has already begun to rely more and more upon himself and not upon any member of his family, no matter how dearly he loves and wants them. His years as a seaman, his more recent work as a reporter and poet are some evidence of this independence. Most of all, his experiences at sea have afforded a few glimpses into the possibility of joy and harmony in life and, even, a sense of "belonging."

EDMUND'S MOMENTS OF PEACE

Appropriately, Edmund describes this vision to his father late that night during a moment of unusual confidence between them. He tells of the time when, on an old square rigger bound for Buenos Aires, lying alone on the bowsprit in the moonlight, he "became drunk with the beauty and singing rhythm" of the ship and for a moment lost himself utterly.

> I was set free! I dissolved in the sea, became white sails and flying spray, became beauty and rhythm and became moonlight and the ship and the high dim-starred sky! I belonged, without past or future, within peace and unity and a wild joy, within something greater than my own life, or the life of Man, to Life Itself! To God, if you want to put it that way.

Another time, aloft in the crow's nest of a steamship, he again knew the ecstasy and release, again experienced "the peace, the end of the quest, the last harbor, the joy of belonging to a fulfillment beyond men's lousy, pitiful, greedy fears and hopes and dreams!" These moments were, as Edmund realizes, comparable to "a saint's vision of beatitude," when the veil of things is suddenly drawn back.

> For a second you see—and seeing the secret, are the secret. For a second there is meaning! Then the hand lets the veil fall and you are alone, lost in the fog again, and you stumble on toward nowhere, for no good reason!

As against the usual experience of life's meaninglessness, its absurdity, these moments of mystic insight, of oneness and wholeness and harmony, of man's being at home in the universe, stand out sharply. The passage clearly links O'Neill to the great romantics, such as Wordsworth, and against those with whom he is more generally associated and whom Edmund much enjoys reading or quoting: Nietzsche, Baudelaire, Strindberg. Edmund's visions, however, are extremely brief—as brief as they are rare. The question becomes, Are they powerful enough to sustain him or anyone else so beset with ill health and loneliness and a strong sense of his own unworthiness and unwantedness?

O'NEILL'S AUTOBIOGRAPHICAL INFLUENCE

The ending suggests a pretty definite negative, but for a more complete answer it is necessary to move out of the play and into the autobiographical matrix from which it emerged. As his various biographers have shown, O'Neill was beset by exactly these sorts of obstacles. Like Edmund, he was "a stranger who never feels at home . . . who can never belong, who must always be a little in love with death." What saved him from complete self-destruction was undoubtedly his instinct for self-preservation coupled with an essential toughness, but also the beginning of his commitment to writing. Though the fictional Edmund regards himself as no true poet and his inspired speech to his father as mere "stammering," the "native eloquence of us fog people," the real O'Neill's devotion to his art not only produced astonishing plays, but gave him a "home," a focus for his life such as no place or person—not even, perhaps, his third wife Carlotta, who bears the glowing dedication of this play—could ever provide him with for so long or so well. Such glimpses as Edmund has had into the beautiful harmony of the universe may otherwise be available, then, at least since the decline of religion in the West, only in art (as E.M. Forster has said), in the making of fictions, where man can create the kinds of unity and coherence and, hence, meaningfulness that actual life insistently appears to deny.

Alcoholism and Addiction in *Long Day's Journey into Night*

Steven F. Bloom

Every character in *Long Day's Journey into Night* ingests some kind of intoxicant; and the four major characters are addicted. Steven F. Bloom argues that the alcoholic's desire to transcend or escape a painful reality reflects O'Neill's vision of the modern human condition. Bloom indicates that beneath the calm facade and false tranquility of the first act are deep tensions within the Tyrone household, namely defensiveness, nervousness, and anger. These tensions are heightened by the inability of the Tyrones to communicate meaningfully.

The center of the family's dysfunction is the wife and mother, Mary. Bloom writes that the family, in an attempt to cover up Mary's morphine addiction, has adopted a pattern of denial. Bloom suggests that the father and sons displace their anger toward Mary and direct it at each other. Their denial and anger, in turn, lead to more drinking and feed their own alcoholic addiction. It is a spiral that the Tyrones are unable to break.

Steven F. Bloom is a professor of English at Emmanuel College in Boston. He has published several articles on O'Neill.

One of the most pervasive critical comments about much of Eugene O'Neill's drama is that it is repetitious. Some critics recognize that this repetitiousness is essential to the dramatist's vision, especially in the late plays, yet few seem to appreciate the vital connection between the repetitiousness, the vision, and alcoholism. The life of an alcoholic, after all, is very much defined by repetitious behavioral patterns, and it is in these patterns—in the symptoms and effects of alcoholism—that O'Neill finally discovered a realistic context in which to dramatize his vision of life.

ALCOHOLIC BEHAVIOR

In *Long Day's Journey into Night,* the realities of alcoholism are vividly depicted in the behavioral patterns of the Tyrone family, collectively and individually, and especially in the dissipation of Jamie Tyrone and the disintegration of Mary Tyrone. Edmund is the romantic idealist, whose visions of transcendence are pointedly couched in terms of romantic notions of blissful intoxication. In the contrast between this romantic myth of intoxication and the realistic symptoms and effects of alcoholism, O'Neill captures the despairing paradox of the human condition, as he sees it.

Three of the four major characters in *Long Day's Journey* become intoxicated by Act IV; the fourth character is under the influence of morphine throughout most of the play. The only other character, Cathleen the servant, is actually drunk most of the brief time she is onstage. Everyone in the play, then, ingests some kind of intoxicant, and the four major characters are, to varying degrees, addicted. This pervasive dependence on chemical substances inevitably affects the behavior of the characters and their interactions in various ways, some subtle and some blatant.

It is important that the symptoms of alcoholism are commonly identified with the symptoms of addiction to chemical substances in general, and that the term "chemical dependency" is used interchangeably with "alcoholism" and "addiction." Furthermore, many of the symptoms of "opioid intoxication" (and morphine is an opioid) are often easily confused with those of alcoholic intoxication. So although Mary Tyrone is addicted to morphine rather than to alcohol, she can still be considered the central addictive figure within the family, and the behavior of this family can be viewed as typical of families of chemically-dependent individuals.

The Diagnostic and Statistical Manual of Mental Disorders (DSM-III) describes the behavioral disorders caused by opioid dependence as being "marked by remissions while in treatment or prison or when the substance is scarce and [by] relapses on returning to a familiar environment where these substances are available and friends or colleagues use these substances." Mary Tyrone is at just such a juncture when this play begins; we eventually discover that she has recently returned from a sanatorium, and that her addictive behavior has been in remission. Her home environment, however, is clearly established as one that is highly conducive to relapse. The Tyrone men may have a different "substance of choice," but their dependence on alcohol obviously reinforces Mary's inclination to return to morphine. In addition, the apparent isolation of the Tyrones from external influences of any kind increases the chances of relapse for Mary.

DENIAL IN THE FAMILY SYSTEM

Within this environment, however, the family has success-fully created a façade of calm and pleasant normality. It is in the elaborate system of denial with which they have fostered this smooth surface that the Tyrones initially appear to fit the mold of the "alcoholic family." In an article called "The Progression of Alcoholism and the Family," Don and Nancy Howard[1] point out that in the constant attempt to deny that there is a problem in the family, the alcoholic and his or her relatives will "establish themselves in routines and patterns of communication that appear to work on the surface."

So effective are the patterns and routines established by the Tyrone family that when one first views or reads the play, the true nature of the situation can go unnoticed for a while. Nobody drinks during the first act; there are only a few refer-ences to drinking and drunkenness, and these seem rather innocuous; and certainly, all references to morphine are oblique and evasive. Thus *Long Day's Journey* begins as a pleasant, peaceful domestic drama might begin, quite obvi-ously similar, in fact, to O'Neill's own domestic comedy *Ah, Wilderness!* As Henry Hewes remarked in his review of the original New York production of *Long Day's Journey,* "one might assume that this was going to be a comedy about two 'regular fellers' and their happily-married mom and dad." It is morning; the family has had breakfast; Tyrone and Mary enter together smiling and teasing each other quite lovingly, with the two sons heard laughing in the dining room. Little is missing, it seems, from the scene of domestic tranquility. As the act progresses, however, we notice hints that all is not well beneath the surface, and that the three men are desperately trying to sustain the calm façade.

---

1. therapists

The earliest indications of tensions are not directly, explicitly, connected to alcoholism. There is apparently a generational conflict between the father and his two sons, but at first this hardly seems remarkable; there is also obvious concern for Edmund's health and Mary's "nervousness," but the latter is not necessarily drug-related. There is certainly a pattern of defensiveness within the family, as hardly a comment goes by without provoking a defensive reaction from someone. Even Edmund's story about Shaughnessy and the pigs—the kind of story O'Neill often uses in his plays to promote an atmosphere of camaraderie—here leads to an argument with the father pitted against his two sons. For the most part, however, the men make concerted efforts to contain their arguments and to sustain a jocular and amiable atmosphere. That it *is* an effort to do so becomes clear as soon as Mary exits; then, the façade falls and the mood changes drastically.

ANGER AND DEFENSIVENESS

The anger and defensiveness beneath the surface are now released in a confrontation between father and son that consists of bitter accusations and counteraccusations. The contrast between this scene and the previous one when Mary was present illustrates a pattern within the alcoholic family that the Howards describe as typical:

> If the problem drinker appears to be in a pleasant mood and is sober, no one would dare mention anything unpleasant or any drinking behavior, fearing that such a communication would rock the boat and the pleasant mood would be drowned in the resulting anger and defensive response.

Thus, the anger and defensiveness that are suppressed in Mary's presence later emerge, displaced into other issues and other relationships. So, rather than discussing their feelings about Mary's addiction and the family's problems in any sustained and meaningful way, the two men argue about other matters. Jamie blames his father for Edmund's illness because, he says, Tyrone has hired the doctor who charges the least to treat him; and Tyrone responds to this by admonishing his son for wasting his life and for being ungrateful. Once again, the observations of the Howards are germane:

> Each person keeps the cycle revolving with denial, fear, guilt, blame, confusion and belief in myths. In this kind of family, communication is vague, unclear, and indirect; roles are

upset and inconsistent and rules are unspoken and broken; self-worth is negative and low; and the total atmosphere is distrustful and closed.

This description seems made to order for the interactions we observe among the Tyrones throughout Act I.

THE BREAKDOWN OF COMMUNICATION

An important example of the lack of communication in the Tyrone family occurs in this scene between Jamie and Tyrone. Tyrone accuses his son of ingratitude in the following terms: "The only thanks is to have you sneer at me for a dirty miser, sneer at my profession, sneer at every damn thing in the world except yourself." Significantly, Jamie denies this: "That's not true, Papa. You can't hear me talking to myself, that's all." Jamie's wry confession of his self-hatred is a clear indication of what lies beneath the sneering persona he presents to the world; it is a glimpse of the self-loathing that he will confess painfully in Act IV. Most significantly here, however, it is a comment that goes virtually unnoticed by his father, who merely *stares at him, puzzledly, then quotes mechanically* ": "'Ingratitude, the vilest weed that grows'!" Tyrone does not hear the self-hatred in his son's words; he hears only what he customarily expects to hear—ingratitude. In addition, Jamie's response to his father's quotation further confirms the impression that their argument conforms to a pattern, even down to the details of the literary allusions: "I could see that line coming! God, how many thousand times—! *He stops, bored with their quarrel, and shrugs his shoulders.* All right, Papa. I'm a bum. Anything you like, so long as it stops the argument." The pattern is predictable and they barely feel the need to listen to each other anymore.

MOMENTS OF COMPASSION

Within this pattern of hostile defensiveness, however, there are moments of genuine, mutual concern and compassion. O'Neill describes one of these moments of "understanding sympathy": "It is as if suddenly a deep bond of common feeling existed between them [James and Jamie] in which their antagonisms could be forgotten." Although it is only momentary, this shared sympathy does exist, and it should remain a constant factor beneath all of the arguments and accusations. These peaceful moments of mutual compassion, and the suggestion that these feelings always exist, should establish the bonds that tie these people together. Although they are unable to live with each other in tranquility, they are even less capable of living without each other. This familial loyalty is certainly not an uncommon feature in alcoholic families: although they cause each other tremendous suffering, the family members remain loyal at each other. The problem is not whether or not they care about each other, but rather, the difficulty they have expressing the caring feelings and acting on them in a helpful way.

So it is also typical that these moments of compassion inevitably give way to continuation of hostilities, as we observe here in the case of the Tyrones. After the resumption of hostilities between father and son, we are reminded of the extent to which their behavior revolves around the central addictive personality—the wife-mother. When she enters the room, the men's hostility changes to feigned heartiness and cheer. . . .

As James and Jamie increasingly suspect Mary's relapse, they try to cover up any indications of hostility between them that might upset her. It quickly becomes evident, however, that the attempt to sustain the calm atmosphere, given the feelings of guilt and blame, is a formidable task. Certainly, the movement of much of the first three acts of *Long Day's Journey* follows this path over these hills and into the valleys, and they are the same hills and valleys traversed again and again. In terms of the accompanying image, the "egg shells" in the Tyrone family are pervasive; they surround each character. Indeed, Act I could appropriately be subtitled, "Walking on Egg Shells."

MARY TYRONE'S ADDICTIVE BEHAVIOR

An important factor in the cycle, of course, is the behavior of the addict—in this case, Mary. Throughout the first act, her behavior is rather mysterious; she is clearly troubled, yet her sons and husband do not acknowledge this impression in any explicit way. They attempt only to ignore it, or to put a positive light on what they, and we, see:

> JAMIE. *With an awkward, uneasy tenderness.* We're all so proud of you, Mama, so darned happy. *She stiffens and stares at him with a frightened defiance. He flounders on.* But you've still got to be careful. You mustn't worry so much about Edmund. He'll be all right.

MARY. *With a stubborn, bitterly resentful look.* Of course, he'll be all right. And I don't know what you mean.

JAMIE. *Rebuffed and hurt, shrugs his shoulders.* All right, Mama. I'm sorry I spoke.

The denial system is illustrated here quite clearly, both on the level of Jamie's denial of their fears about what seems to be happening to her, and on the level of Mary's denial. Even when presented with the indirect concern for her in terms of Edmund's condition, she is stubbornly resistant to acknowledging any problem at all. Her bitter resentment confirms the sense of necessity that the men feel to avoid even the most oblique reference to her condition. And Jamie's attempt to express concern actually suggests his own desire to believe that his mother is not experiencing a relapse. Her denial that there is anything for her to "be careful" about obviously implies that indeed there is: the denial is symptomatic of the disease.

In the following scene between Mary and Edmund, we move closer towards perceiving the truth about the situation. Naturally, mother and son attempt to sustain the façade of pleasant amiability, which inevitably evolves into the usual cycle of accusation, guilty defensiveness, and counter-accusation. As Mary becomes increasingly desperate, she finally attempts to blame the cycle itself:

MARY. Oh, I can't bear it, Edmund, when even you—! *Her hands flutter up to pat her hair in their aimless distracted way. Suddenly a strange undercurrent of revengefulness comes into her voice.* It would serve all of you right if it was true!

These words suggest that Mary is looking for the justification she feels she needs to resume her drug addiction. This is, of course, typical of the rationalization process observed in alcoholics. At this point, Mary manages to turn the men's suspicious concern for her around and make it a reason for her relapse. Her revengefulness now becomes part of the pattern; she now has a way to blame *them* for the current situation. . . .

When Tyrone is confronted with the undeniable evidence of his wife's relapse, his countenance noticeably changes and he appears to be a "tired, bitterly sad old man." In his anger and disappointment, he turns to alcohol; the intense stress of confronting the truth is apparent as he pours his second drink and Mary comments that he never has "more than one before lunch":

MARY. . . . I know what to expect. You will be drunk tonight. Well, it won't be the first time, will it—or the thousandth?

The circular nature of their predicament is reiterated here: Tyrone uses Mary's relapse as an excuse to drink, while she uses his drinking as an excuse for her relapse. The rationalization process is typical, as are the pleas for help and defensive denials that operate in the scene between husband and wife as they seek and find more justification for their addictive behavior.

By the beginning of Act II, Scene ii, Mary has clearly resumed taking the morphine and the others know it. When they enter, therefore, although the situation is parallel to the opening scene of the play, the contrast is striking. Now, they are merely going through the motions of domestic normalcy. Tyrone enters behind his wife, not with her, and he "avoids touching her or looking at her." The sons are no longer joking and laughing, but rather, "Jamie's face is hard with defensive cynicism," and Edmund is "heartsick as well as physically ill." Mary is discussing domestic matters, but this time nobody listens to her, and she herself seems "indifferent." While Mary continues to deny her relapse, the others find it increasingly difficult to do so; thus, they fluctuate between bitter denial and resigned acceptance, with Edmund the most resistant. All attempts to sustain the semblance of domestic tranquility of Act I have been dropped.

As Mary becomes increasingly intoxicated, she retreats further into the past, where she finds familiar disappointments to weave into the pattern of guilt and blame. For instance, she blames James for not providing a home for her, suggesting that this deprivation has been a cause of her addiction; in response, James blames her addiction for rendering it impossible to maintain a "real home." Neither of them accepts the other's accusations, on the surface, yet their defensiveness implies at least a subconscious sense of responsibility. Mary claims, though, that she is not bitter, that it is not James' fault; however, she does not accept the responsibility herself. Instead, the implication is that nobody is responsible, which means, of course, that there is nothing anyone can do about the situation. The addictive personality typically relinquishes responsibility for his or her behavior, which fosters the addiction. As we see again and again, this attitude defines life for Mary Tyrone.

Meanwhile, the beliefs of the father and sons are increasingly tested by Mary's retreat to addiction. Jamie is increasingly cynical, at this point accepting his mother's relapse as total: "They never come back." On the other hand, Edmund remains desperately optimistic: "It can't have got a hold on her yet. She can still stop." It is typical of Tyrone's misunderstanding of his sons that he rejects both of their philosophies as being equally "rotten to the core," when, in fact, they are different.

Edmund continues to speak of communicating with Mary, while his father and brother are prepared to accept the next stage of her progression:

> JAMIE. *Shrugs his shoulders.* You can't talk to her now. She'll listen but she won't listen. She'll be here but she won't be here. You know the way she gets.
>
> TYRONE. Yes, that's the way the poison acts on her always. Every day from now on, there'll be the same drifting away from us until by the end of each night—

Edmund cannot tolerate this challenge to his beliefs, so he characteristically avoids any additional disturbing conversation by leaving the room. This allows the other two—Jamie and James—to confront each other and the situation, about which they seem to agree. In spite of their awareness of the facts, however, their confrontation again becomes an occasion for the expression of disappointment and anger that is displaced onto each other rather than directed towards Mary, or towards themselves. Each feels guilty about Mary's relapse, and each also blames the other. The feelings are played out, however, in terms of Edmund's illness and what will be done for him now that the doctor has diagnosed consumption. Jamie accuses his father of putting monetary considerations before Edmund's best interests, and Tyrone retaliates by insinuating once again that it is Jamie's influence on Edmund that has made him vulnerable to the disease. This argument allows them to avoid the issue of Mary's addiction, and eventually it redirects their attention to Jamie's drinking, a related issue, but one that is regarded as a less serious one by this family.

There is, of course, sufficient evidence in the play that the Tyrone men are alcoholics. The description of Jamie when he first appears mentions "signs of premature disintegration" and "marks of dissipation," key words in O'Neill's descriptions of alcoholic characters in his other plays. Jamie, then, seems to be the most visibly affected by his addiction, on a physical level. There have been other signs, though, of dependency in all three of them. The drinks before lunch, the sneaking of drinks behind Tyrone's back, Cathleen's comments about their drinking habits, all clearly indicate alcoholic dependence. Furthermore, Tyrone's constant refrain that he has "never missed a performance" sounds very much like the typical attempt by the alcoholic to convince others that he has no drinking problem. Whether or not he has ever missed a performance is irrelevant. There is sufficient evidence that he drinks heavily, and behaves irresponsibly because of it, as Mary's story of their honeymoon suggests. The fact, however, that he feels the need to "prove" that he does not have a problem is his indictment. And when he says that "no man has ever had a better reason [to get drunk]," this is the symptomatic rationalization system of the addictive personality. . . .

In *Long Day's Journey into Night*, O'Neill captures his vision of the human condition in the figure of the alcoholic who is constantly and repeatedly faced with the disappointment of his hopes to escape or transcend present reality. As the effects of heavy drinking and alcoholism increase, the alcoholic, in his attempt to attain euphoric forgetfulness, is repeatedly confronted with the painful realities of dissipation, despondency, self-destruction, and ultimately, death. This is the life of an alcoholic, and for O'Neill, this is the life of modern man.

Family Connections in *Long Day's Journey into Night*

Robert Brustein

According to Robert Brustein, the members of the Tyrone family in *Long Day's Journey into Night* are intertwined, the behavior of one often unwittingly causing pain or resentment in the others. Brustein explains that the Tyrones are also victims of the past; the transgressions of earlier generations seep into the present as guilt and blame. In an attempt to find comfort, each family member turns to dreams and nostalgia. O'Neill uses the images of light, dark, fog, and mist to convey this sense of journeying into the past; each character withdraws into the "fog" to mask the pain of the present. Brustein suggests that this autobiographical play is O'Neill's vehicle to forgive his own family and reconcile himself to his own past.

Robert Brustein is a professor of English at Harvard University. He is also an actor, drama critic for the *London Observer*, and artistic director of the American Repertory Theatre Company. His works include *Critical Moments: Reflections on Theatre and Society, The Cultural Watch: Essays on Theatre and Society*, and *Revolution as Theatre: Notes on the Radical Style*. He is a contributor of articles and reviews to numerous periodicals.

In *Long Day's Journey*, O'Neill has dismissed . . . superficial concerns to concentrate on the deeper implications of his theme: what is visited on the sons is a strain of blank misfortune. Here is a family living in a close symbiotic relationship, a single organism with four branches, where a twitch in one creates a spasm in another. O'Neill was beginning to explore this kind of relationship in *The Iceman Cometh*, where the derelicts aggravate each other's agony and hell is other people, but here he has worked out the nightmare of family relations with relentless precision. No individual character trait is revealed which does not have a bearing on the lives of the entire family; the play is nothing but the truth, but there is nothing irrelevant in the play. Thus, the two major characteristics which define James Tyrone, Sr.—his miserliness and his career as an actor—are directly related to the misery of his wife and children. Tyrone's niggardliness has caused Mary's addiction, because it was a cut-rate quack doctor who first introduced her to drugs; and Tyrone's inability to provide her with a proper home, because he was always on the road, has intensified her bitterness and sense of loss. The miser in Tyrone is also the source of Edmund's resentment, since Tyrone is preparing to send him to a State Farm for treatment instead of to a more expensive rest home. Edmund's tuberculosis, in turn, partially accounts for Mary's resumption of her habit, because she cannot face the fact of his bad health; and Edmund's birth caused the illness which eventually introduced his mother to drugs. Jamie is affected by the very existence of Edmund, since his brother's literary gifts fill him with envy and a sense of failure; and his mother's inability to shake her habit has made him lose faith in his own capacity for regeneration. Even the comic touches are structured along causal lines: Tyrone is too cheap to burn the lights in the parlor, so Edmund bangs his knee on a hatstand, and Jamie stumbles on the steps. Every action has a radiating effect, and characters interlock in the manner which evoked the anguished cry from Strindberg:[1] "Earth, earth is hell . . . in which I cannot move without injuring the happiness of others, in which others cannot remain happy without hurting me."

The family, in brief, is chained together by resentment, guilt, recrimination; yet, the chains that hold it are those of love as well as hate. Each makes the other suffer through some unwitting act, a breach of love or faith, and reproaches follow furiously in the wake of every revelation. But even at the moment that the truth is being blurted out, an apologetic retraction is being formed. Nobody really desires to

---

1. Swedish playwright August

hurt. Compassion and understanding alternate with anger and rancor. Even Jamie, who is "forever making sneering fun of somebody" and who calls his mother a "hophead," hates his own bitterness and mockery, and is filled with self-contempt. The four members of the family react to each other with bewildering ambivalence—exposing illusions and sustaining them, striking a blow and hating the hand that strikes. Every torment is self-inflicted, every angry word reverberating in the conscience of the speaker. It is as if the characters existed only to torture each other, while protecting each other, too, against their own resentful tongues.

THE INFLUENCE OF THE PAST

There is a curse on the blighted house of the Tyrones, and the origin of the curse lies elsewhere, with existence itself. As Mary says, "None of us can help the things life has done to us." In tracing down the origin of this curse, O'Neill has returned to the year 1912; but as the play proceeds, he brings us even further into the past. Implicated in the misfortunes of the house are not only the two generations of Tyrones, but a previous generation as well; Edmund's attempted suicide, before the action begins, is linked to the suicide of Tyrone's father, and Edmund's consumption is the disease by which Mary's father died. Though O'Neill does not mention this, the tainted legacy reaches into the future, too: the play-wright's elder son, Eugene Jr., is also to commit suicide, and his younger son, Shane, is to become, like his grandmother, a narcotics addict. The generations merge, and so does Time. "The past is the present, isn't it?" cries Mary. "It's the future too. We all try to lie out of that but life won't let us."

O'Neill, the probing artist, seeks in the past for the origination of guilt and blame; but his characters seek happiness and dreams. All four Tyrones share an intense hatred of the present and its morbid, inescapable reality. All four seek solace from the shocks of life in nostalgic memories, which they reach through different paths. For Mary, the key that turns the lock of the past is morphine. "It kills the pain. You go back until at last you are beyond its reach. Only the past when you were happy is real." The pain she speaks of is in her crippled hands, the constant reminder of her failed dream to be a concert pianist, but even more it is in her crippled, guilty soul. Mary has betrayed all her hopes and dreams. Even her marriage is a betrayal, since she longed to be a nun, wholly dedicated to her namesake, the Blessed Virgin; but her addiction betrays her religion, family, and home. She cannot pray; she is in a state of despair; and the accusations of her family only aggravate her guilt. Mary is subject to a number of illusions—among them, the belief that she married beneath her—but unlike the derelicts of *The Iceman,* who dream of the future, she only dreams of the past. Throughout the action, she is trying to escape the pain of the present entirely; and at the end, with the aid of drugs, she has finally returned to the purity, innocence, and hope of her girlhood. Although the title of the play suggests a progress, therefore, the work moves always backwards. The long journey is a journey into the past.

IMAGES OF FOG AND DARKNESS

O'Neill suggests this in many ways, partly through ambiguous images of light and dark, sun and mist. The play begins at 8:30 in the morning with a trace of fog in the air, and concludes sometime after midnight, with the house fog-bound—the mood changing from sunny cheer over Mary's apparent recovery to gloomy despair over her new descent into hell. The nighttime scenes occur logically at the end of the day; but subjectively, the night precedes the day, for the play closes on a phantasmagoria of past time. Under the influence of Mary's drugs—and, to some extent, the alcohol of the men—time evaporates and hovers, and disappears: past, present, future become one. Mary drifts blissfully into illusions under cover of the night, which functions like a shroud against the harsh, daylight reality. And so does that fog that Mary loves: "It hides you from the world and the world from you," she says. "You feel that everything has changed, and nothing is what it seemed to be. No one can find or touch you any more." Her love for her husband and children neutralized by her terrible sense of guilt, Mary withdraws more and more into herself. And this, in turn, intensifies the unhappiness of the men: "The hardest thing to take," says Edmund, "is the blank wall she builds around herself. Or it's more like a bank of fog in which she hides and loses herself. . . . It's as if, in spite of loving us, she hated us."

Mary, however, is not alone among the "fog people"—the three men also have their reasons for withdrawing into night. Although less shrouded in illusion than Mary, each, nevertheless, haunts the past like a ghost, seeking consolation for a wasted life. For Tyrone, his youth was a period of artistic promise when he had the potential to be a great actor instead of a commercial hack; his favorite memory is of Booth's praising his Othello, words which he has written down and lost. For Jamie, who might have borne the Tyrone name "in honor and dignity, who showed such brilliant promise," the present is without possibility; he is now a hopeless ne'er-do-well, pursuing oblivion in drink and the arms of fat whores while mocking his own failure in bathetic, self-hating accents: "My name is Might-Have-Been," he remarks, quoting from Rossetti, "I am also called No More, Too Late, Farewell." For Edmund, who is more like his mother than the others, night and fog are a refuge from the curse of living:

> The fog was where I wanted to be. . . . That's what I wanted—to be alone with myself in another world where truth is untrue and life can hide from itself. . . . It was like walking on the bottom of the sea. As if I had drowned long ago. As if I was a ghost belonging to the fog, and the fog was the ghost of the sea. It felt damned peaceful to be nothing more than a ghost within a ghost.

Reality, truth, and life plague him like a disease. Ashamed of being human, he finds existence itself detestable: "Who wants to see life as it is, if they can help it? It's the three Gorgons in one. You look in their faces and die. Or it's Pan. You see him and die—that is, inside you—and have to go on living as a ghost."

"We are such stuff as manure is made on, so let's drink up and forget it"—like Strindberg, who developed a similar excremental view of humankind, the young Edmund has elected to withdraw from Time by whatever means available, and one of these is alcohol. Edmund, whose taste in poetry is usually execrable, finally quotes a good poet, Baudelaire,[2] on the subject of drunkenness: "Be drunken, if you would not be martyred slaves of Time; be drunken continually! With wine, with poetry, or with virtue, as you will." And in order to avoid being enslaved by Time, Edmund contemplates other forms of drunkenness as well. In his fine fourth-act speech, he tells of his experiences at sea, when he discovered Nirvana for a moment, pulling out of Time and dissolving into the infinite:

2. French poet Charles Pierre

> I belonged, without past or future, within peace and unity
> and a wild joy, within something greater than my own life, or
> the life of Man, to Life itself! To God, if you want to put it that
> way. . . . For a second you see—and seeing the secret, are the
> secret. For a second there is meaning! Then the hand lets the
> veil fall and you are alone, lost in the fog again, and you stum-
> ble on towards nowhere, for no good reason.

The ecstatic vision of wholeness is only momentary, and
Edmund, who "would have been more successful as a sea-
gull or a fish," must once again endure the melancholy fate
of living in reality: "As it is, I will always be a stranger who
never feels at home, who does not really want and is not
really wanted, who can never belong, who must always be a
little in love with death!" In love with death since death is
the ultimate escape from Time, the total descent into night
and fog.

THE PLAY AS O'NEILL'S CONFESSION

There is a fifth Tyrone involved in the play—the older
Eugene O'Neill. And although he has superimposed his later
on his earlier self (Edmund, described as a socialist and
atheist, has many religious-existential attitudes), the author
and the character are really separable. Edmund wishes to
deny Time, but O'Neill has elected to return to it once again—
reliving the past and mingling with his ghosts—in order to
find the secret and meaning of their suffering. For the playwright has discovered another escape besides alcohol,
Nirvana, or death from the terrible chaos of life: the escape
of art where chaos is ordered and the meaningless made
meaningful. The play itself is an act of forgiveness and reconciliation, the artist's lifelong resentment disintegrated
through complete understanding of the past and total self-
honesty.

These qualities dominate the last act, which proceeds
through a sequence of confessions and revelations to a harrowing climax. Structurally, the act consists of two long col-
loquies—the first between Tyrone and Edmund, the second
between Edmund and Jamie—followed by a long soliloquy
from Mary who, indeed, concludes every act. Tyrone's confession of failure as an actor finally makes him understand-
able to Edmund who thereupon forgives him all his faults;
and Jamie's confession of his ambivalent feelings towards
his brother, and his half-conscious desire to make him fail
too, is the deepest psychological moment in the play. But the

most honest moment of self-revelation occurs at the end of Edmund's speech, after he has tried to explain the origin of his bitterness and despair. Tyrone, as usual, finds his son's musings "morbid," but he has to admit that Edmund has "the makings of a poet." Edmund replies:

> The *makings* of a poet. No, I'm afraid I'm like the guy who is always panhandling for a smoke. He hasn't even got the makings. He's got only the habit. I couldn't touch what I tried to tell you just now. I just stammered. That's the best I'll ever do. . . . Well, it will be faithful realism, at least. Stammering is the native eloquence of us fog people.

In describing his own limitations as a dramatist, O'Neill here rises to real eloquence; speaking the truth has given him a tongue. Having accepted these limitations, and dedicated himself to a "faithful realism" seen through the lens of the "family kodak," he has turned into a dramatist of the very first rank.

Character Conflicts in *A Moon for the Misbegotten*

Doris V. Falk

A Moon for the Misbegotten presents the story of James Tyrone Jr., who is based on O'Neill's older brother, James Jr. Doris V. Falk writes that the play has two parts: farce in act 1 and tragedy through the rest of the drama. The farce becomes tragic when O'Neill reveals the sadness and humiliation of the two main characters, Josie and Tyrone. Both of them suffer from an internal psychological battle that veers between self-hatred and neurotic pride. Falk argues that Josie suffers with this conflict but can still manage to find some value in her life. Tyrone, however, cannot deal with the tension and is devastated by guilt and hopelessness. Falk suggests that Tyrone is like many of O'Neill's male characters who hate the things they love, act rebelliously, and ultimately end up despising themselves. At the end of the play, Josie's love for Tyrone offers him relief from himself so that he can sleep and die, comforted like a lost little boy who has finally found his mother.

Doris Falk is a teacher of English and a professor emeritus at Douglas College of Rutgers University, New Brunswick, New Jersey. She is the author of *Lillian Hellman*.

The sequel to *Long Day's Journey*, *A Moon for the Misbegotten*, continues the story of James Tyrone, Jr., who represents O'Neill's older brother, James, Jr. In *Long Day's Journey*, "Jamie" is an alcoholic, seeking constant escape from his own inadequacies and from guilt toward his younger brother and his mother. His final refuge is in lechery, but he can find satisfaction only in ugly, oversized women, the prostitutes rejected

Excerpted from *Eugene O'Neill and the Tragic Tension: An Interpretive Study of the Plays* by Doris V. Falk. Copyright © 1958 by Rutgers, The State University. Reprinted by permission of Rutgers University Press.

by other men, who feed his self-hatred and his need for a mother-substitute. The love affair in *A Moon for the Misbegotten* is derived from *Long Day's Journey*, which defines Jamie's love, hatred, and guilt toward his mother and the desperate longing for her which drives him to Josie in *Moon*.

FARCE AND TRAGEDY

If *A Moon for the Misbegotten* is a part of James, Jr.'s biography, then as biography, it is a thing of pity and terror. But as drama, it is the veriest scratching in rat's alley. The first half (actually Act I) is a crude country-bumpkin farce, taking place outside the run-down shack of a tenant farmer in Connecticut. In the second half, as in *Iceman*, "the comedy breaks up and the tragedy comes on." The change in tenor is simply a change in point of view. The setting of Act II is "the same, but with the interior of sitting room revealed"— and the interior of the characters also. Before, they were comic grotesques, seen by a detached observer; now they are revealed from their own subjective point of view as pathetic creatures of "sadness and loneliness and humiliation."

Pathos cannot save *A Moon for the Misbegotten* (New York, 1952) from the weakness of its outward situation—the theatrical cliché of clichés, for which there is no other word but corn. O'Neill added a few twists, anecdotes, and complications for interest and transition to the psychological, but the skeletal story concerns the attempt of the farmer and the farmer's daughter to save the old homestead from the clutches of a supposedly villainous landlord. To this antiquity, like insult to injury, O'Neill has added another: the vaudeville team of the big strong woman who chases a puny man around the stage with (a) a broom and (b) the threat of a smothering embrace in a pair of enormous arms and an appalling bosom. The crowning indignity is the use, as a sort of refrain, of the maudlin sob-tune, "My mother's in the baggage coach ahead." Thus the play begins with a minstrel show (there actually exists a minstrel tune that goes, "A mother was chasing her boy with a broom, she was chasing her boy 'round the room. . . .") and ends with meller-drammer. And with all his early theatrical experience and his belief that "life copies melodrama," O'Neill certainly knew what he was doing. He drops us a hint when he has Hogan, the farmer, describe his scheme for trapping the landlord (forcing him into a shotgun wedding with his daughter): "It's as old as the hills. . . . But . . . sometimes an old trick is best because it's so ancient no one would suspect you'd try it."

A PSYCHOLOGICAL PATTERN IN THE PLAY

As to the serious, or "subjective," side of the play, the revelations of the psychological problems of the characters fit perfectly—too perfectly—into the pattern of O'Neill's thought at this time: that balance between the opposite masks of self, that paralyzing suspension of all value, which is fatal to action and movement and signifies the end of life. This pattern is actually all there is to the play; for, whereas *The Iceman Cometh* has a story and reveals living characters in conflict with themselves and each other, the story of *A Moon for the Misbegotten* serves only as a rack on which to hang—or stretch—the unconverted symbols of neurosis.

The three central characters of this play are New England Irish, with just enough Catholicism still clinging to them to provide expressive profanity. Phil Hogan is the farmer, his daughter is Josie, and Jim Tyrone, Jr., is the landlord whose family has long owned the Hogan farm. Hogan is a buffoon with a shrewd, coarse sense of humor but a soft heart, who serves in the plot largely as a kind of *deus ex machina* to bring the lovers together. On the pretext that Tyrone is planning to sell the farm to a neighboring villainous "Standard Oil man," Hogan persuades Josie to seduce Tyrone—then to blackmail him, by forcing him either to marry her or to pay Hogan the price of the farm to avoid scandal. However, Hogan reveals later that he knew Tyrone had no intention of selling the farm, and he (Hogan) only wanted to bring the two together so that they would recognize their hidden love for each other—a rather sad piece of hokum.

JOSIE'S INTERNAL CONFLICT

The story belongs, of course, to the misbegotten lovers, Josie, "so oversize for a woman that she is almost a freak," and Tyrone, the hopeless alcoholic, who finds, at least for one night, a mother and a lover in Josie. Unlike the men in *The Iceman Cometh,* Josie and Tyrone are protected by no lasting illusions about themselves. Josie's kindest "pipe dream" is her boast that she is a slut, who has slept with all the men in the neighborhood. But even she is aware of the truth of Jim's accusation that it is her "pride" which makes her affect this pose: that she is actually a virgin, longing to transcend her gross flesh in a spiritual love, but ashamed of this purity which seems too incongruous in a "great, ugly cow" of a woman. When Tyrone attempts to confront Josie with this picture of her "submissive" self as a virgin, she refuses to admit the truth of the picture. To her denial Tyrone replies, "Pride is the sin by which the angels fell. Are you going to keep that up—with me?" O'Neill knew well the close relationship between self-hatred and neurotic pride. To overcome her hatred of that empirical "oversize" self which she can see, Josie has erected a more acceptable one which at least makes her an expansive, forceful character: feeling unlovable, she proves to herself that she can make men desire her, and in that process rejects the mixture of mother and virgin which Tyrone discovers that she really is.

Tyrone reveals Josie's position and his own when he says:

You can take the truth, Josie—from me. Because you and I belong to the same club. We can kid the world but we can't fool ourselves, like most people, no matter what we do—nor escape ourselves no matter where we run away. Whether it's the bottom of a bottle, or a South Sea Island, we'd find our own ghosts there waiting to greet us—"sleepless with pale commemorative eyes," as Rossetti wrote. . . . You don't ask how I saw through your bluff, Josie. You pretend too much.

But Josie is healthy enough to see and accept her conflicting selves for what they are: to be the virgin mother to Tyrone and resume her play-acting role of neighborhood slut when he has gone. She is another Cybel, with enough earthy animal love of life to go on living in spite of her difficulties, to meet the problems of everyday life through the haze of sadness and frustration that hangs over her. She has the "hopeless hope" that springs from Cybel's assumption of the inevitability of life opposites—between which her fate is still suspended, and in which she can still find some value and motion.

TYRONE'S INTERNAL CONFLICT

For Tyrone, on the other hand, there is no hope but in oblivion. He is probably the least dramatic of any of O'Neill's protagonists. His role in the play is one long self-analysis, one endless case history of self-hatred, alienation, neurotic conflict—all within the Oedipus configuration. Tyrone wears the same two masks as Jamie in *Long Day's Journey* (and as John Loving and Dion Anthony). His ravaged face has "a certain Mephisophelean quality which is accentuated by his habitually cynical expression. But when he smiles without sneering, he still has the ghost of a former youthful, irresponsible Irish charm—that of the beguiling ne'er-do-well, sentimental and romantic." In his sodden conversations with Josie he alternates between the coarse cruelty of a disillusioned lecher and the sweetness and simplicity of a little boy crying for his mother. Expansive at one moment, submissive at another, he does not know his real identity and withdraws from both self-images into the oblivion of drunkenness and the darkness of the womb—synonymous for him with tomb.

If the first glimpse of Tyrone reveals his disintegration within the masks of self, the second view of him is a study in self-hatred. At the end of Act II, when he has come to keep a date with Josie (and when *his* intentions are honorable, but hers are to seduce and then blackmail him), he is left for a few minutes alone on the stage.

> TYRONE. *(suddenly, with intense hatred)* You rotten bastard! *(He springs to his feet—fumbles in his pockets for cigarettes—strikes a match which lights up his face, on which there is now an expression of miserable guilt. His hand is trembling so violently he cannot light the cigarette.)*

Tyrone explains his guilt to Josie and to himself in terms of his lifelong hatred of his father and love and guilty longing for his mother. During his father's lifetime Tyrone was a drunkard and a ne'er-do-well, but after his father's death he stopped drinking for his mother's sake. "It made me happy to do it. For her. Because she was all I had, all I cared about. Because I loved her."

Then his mother became ill, and when Tyrone knew she was dying he turned to alcohol again: "I know damned well just before she died she recognized me. She saw I was drunk. Then she closed her eyes so she couldn't see, and was glad to die."

With his mother's death, all purpose and value departed from Tyrone's life, leaving him incapable of emotion, even of grief. He traveled across the country by train with his mother's body "in the baggage coach ahead," and spent his drunken nights with a prostitute he had picked up. Tyrone reduces his motives for this debauchery to vengeance upon his mother for leaving him. From that time on his life has been one long effort to obliterate his guilt and to punish himself not only for his behavior toward his mother, but for his feelings toward her, with their unconscious overtones of incest and hatred. Like so many of O'Neill's men, he hates the thing he loves—rebels against his dependency, then flagellates himself for having desecrated the mother-son (or man-woman) relationship.

JOSIE'S LOVE ABSOLVES TYRONE

When Tyrone comes to Josie, his one desire is for expiation. That same wronged maternal ghost who cried for vindication in *Desire Under the Elms* and *Mourning Becomes Electra* must here again be laid to rest. In Josie's maternal and redemptive love for him Tyrone at last finds forgiveness and release. When he has confessed to Josie and discovers that he is still loved in spite of the hateful self he has revealed in the confession, Tyrone is absolved. The maternal spirit has been placated; now Tyrone can sleep, now he can die. All that remains is the fulfillment of the Earth Mother's final blessing: "May you have your wish and die in your sleep soon, Jim, darling. May you rest forever in forgiveness and peace." *A Moon for the Misbegotten* takes place in September, 1923. O'Neill's brother, James, died on November 8 of that year.

Tyrone is O'Neill's last little boy lost, crying for his mother. Whether or not he actually portrays James O'Neill, Jr., the relationship between him and Josie was O'Neill's final bitter and rather immature comment on the meaning of love. On the application of this view to O'Neill himself, his wife has had the last word. In an interview at the opening of *Long Day's Journey into Night*, Mrs. Carlotta Monterey O'Neill described "Gene's" courtship:

> . . . And he never said to me, "I love you, I think you are wonderful." He kept saying, "I need you, I need you, I need you." And he did need me, I discovered. He was never in good health. He talked about his early life—that he had had no real home, no mother in the real sense, or father, no one to treat him as a child should be treated—and his face became sadder and sadder.

Spiritual Love in *A Moon for the Misbegotten*

Rolf Scheibler

A Moon for the Misbegotten, one of O'Neill's most biographical plays, is his most difficult to stage effectively. Rolf Scheibler argues that the difficulty of the play rests in its mystical quality. He explains that the subtle spiritual connection between the two main characters, Josie and Tyrone, must be so captured by the actors that production does not become sentimental or melodramatic. Josie, the tenant's overweight daughter, desires spiritual love and motherhood but, because of her appearance and insecurities, she hides her feelings behind a mask of wantonness. Tyrone, who represents O'Neill's brother Jamie, also hides behind a mask. Scheibler writes that Tyrone's outward appearance of charm, intellectualism, and strength covers his inward feelings of confusion, inadequacy, and neurosis. In short, Tyrone feels that he has wasted his life and he is seeking forgiveness for his hateful self; he is like a little boy who wants his mother to say everything is all right. According to Scheibler, Tyrone's night with Josie offers some consolation, comfort, and beauty in a world that is harsh and deterministic. Rolf Scheibler holds a doctorate from the University of Basel, Switzerland; this excerpt is part of his dissertation.

MM,[1] completed in 1943 and first produced in Columbus, Ohio, on February 20, 1947, is probably O'Neill's most difficult play from the point of view of the theatre. It is not surprising that it did not prove a success when it was taken on

1. *A Moon for the Misbegotten*

Excerpted from *The Late Plays of Eugene O'Neill* by Rolf Scheibler (Tübingen and Basel: A. Francke, 1970). Reprinted by permission of the publisher.

tour after the first night. In *IC*² the action is still clearly discernible; in *TP*³ the plot is unravelled by a spectacular *coup de théâtre*, and *LDJN*⁴ is enlivened by the continuous bitter quarrels between the members of the Tyrone family. In *MM*, however, the action is supported by a loose framework of comedy, consisting of an intrigue that is not taken seriously even by the characters engaged in it, even their quarrels are never quite genuine; the characters are up to their partners' tricks and launch their verbal battles with gusto. Sometimes they seek to tease each other, sometimes they enjoy the mere fun of the contest, but behind their quarrels we can always feel their purpose of getting closer to each other and of confirming their friendship in their own particular kind of ritual. At the centre of events there is no catastrophe, but a moonlight romance of immense emotional power, which demands delicate and imaginative staging and subtle, intuitive acting if the production is not to become sentimental and melodramatic.

What makes this play difficult, therefore, is not the problem of casting the role of Josie, "so oversize for a woman that she is almost a freak." O'Neill himself dispersed the Theatre Guild's doubts about Mary Welsh, who seemed to be too small for the part; he insisted that she displayed exactly the right "emotional qualities" demanded by this play. This quality he found lacking in James Dunn, who was to play Tyrone and of whom everybody thought that he looked the part. According to [the attorney and business manager of the Washington Square Players Lawrence] Langner "O'Neill kept complaining that Dunn wasn't playing the role with enough gentlemanliness". To Mary Welsh, however, in whose qualities the author trusted from the moment he met her, O'Neill explained what he meant by "emotional qualities". Commenting on why he wanted Irish actors in the cast, he said, "the dry wit, the mercurial changes of mood, the mystic quality of the three main characters are so definitely Irish". It is particularly striking that O'Neill saw a relationship between the terms "mercurial" and "mystic", a relationship that we shall be in a position to confirm further below.

THE MYSTIC QUALITY OF THE PLAY

It is this "mystic quality" which confronts the producer of the play with so many problems. In the central scenes of Acts II

2. *The Iceman Cometh* 3. *A Touch of the Poet* 4. *Long Day's Journey into Night*

and III mood and atmosphere are predominant. Many critics have been completely insensitive in this respect. . . .

Indeed, the critic who is not sensitive to the musical qualities of the play has nothing to seize upon. Doris Falk, who has supplied the most extensive psychoanalytical study of O'Neill's works, does not even think that the characters are of psychological interest. She believes there is evidence in the other late plays that O'Neill successfully converts the characters' mental state into a symbolic one, in which the general situation of modern man is reflected. In *MM*, however, she finds but a case-history realistically presented: ". . . the story of 'A Moon for the Misbegotten' serves only as a rack on which to hang—or stretch—the unconverted symbols of neurosis".

Of course we must protest against such a statement, but we cannot do so by denying the obvious fact that the whole play is permeated with signs of disease and decay. Such qualities are already hinted at in its title, and when the curtain opens, we face a sight of hopeless desolation. The scene is a farm in Connecticut. The dilapidated hut with its ugly one-room annex tacked on to it is in a pitiful state of neglect: the paint has faded and is peeling off, some panes are missing and have been replaced by squares of cardboard. Commenting on the yield of the stone desert, in the midst of which it stands, Hogan, the tenant, sarcastically remarks: "But I have fine reports to give you of a promising harvest. The milkweed and the thistles is in thriving condition, and I never saw the poison ivy so bounteous and beautiful".

The people who live here are, as it were, weeds, too (i.e. misbegotten). Hogan is a cunning and tyrannical drunkard who gains our affection only because he bears his destiny with equanimity and humour. In fact, however, he is a self-indulgent lackadaisical man, "the typical New Irishman, the avaricious, stubborn and unskilful farmer who is unsuccessful in spite of his drudgery". Mary McCarthy is right in pointing out that no normal human being could possibly wish to abide here: Mike's desertion at the beginning of the play underlines this fact and already expresses in theatrical terms that we are to leave the world of everyday life behind us in the course of events: the situation is extraordinary both in respect of the characters' mental state and, as we shall see later, of our own feelings.

JOSIE'S CHARACTER

Josie, the tenant's daughter, is the only figure in the play who is equal to this situation of decay and corruption. Being "more powerful than any but an exeptionally strong man" and having inherited her father's wit, she has no difficulty in keeping her father under control. Her real struggle is fought within herself, for she finds it difficult to accept "the big, great, ugly cow of a woman" she feels herself to be. Her outward appearance seems incompatible with her maidenly desire for spiritual love and motherhood. She therefore hides from the others and from herself behind the mask of the "slut", boasting that she has slept with all the men in the neighbourhood. Her purity, however, remains visible to the spectator throughout the play: Tyrone betrays her lies when he says, "You pretend too much". And we realize that her mask is the device of her "earthy animal love of life", which, according to Doris Falk, enables her "to go on living in spite of her difficulties to meet the problems of everyday life through the haze of sadness and frustration that hangs over her". Her mask is her way of accepting reality, her way of renouncing her deepest personal wishes, and thus deriving some satisfaction from life. Her mask anticipates her action at the climax of the play, where she sacrifices her hope of becoming Tyrone's wife in order to become the mother and virgin mistress he wants her to be. Once more O'Neill's women prove to be stronger, more viable than the men. In this respect Josie resembles Nora and Sara as well as such figures as Cybel in *The Great God Brown.*

TYRONE'S CHARACTER

While Hogan is a failure in a materialistic sense and Josie doomed because of her body, Tyrone is the victim of a purely spiritual conflict. Of the three main characters he is the one who has fallen lowest in spite of the fact that his outward appearance still bears some traces of his former strength and charm.

> His naturally fine physique has become soft and soggy from dissipation, but his face is still good-looking despite its unhealthy puffiness and the bags under the eyes . . . But when he smiles without sneering, he still has the ghost of a former youthful, irresponsible Irish charm—that of the beguiling ne'er-do-well, sentimental and romantic . . . He is dressed in an expensive dark-brown suit. . . .

Tyrone is an intelligent man, who could have proved a gifted scholar if he had not been thrown out of the Jesuit college because of a gross misdemeanour. He still exhibits some signs of learning: he can quote Latin verse, is familiar with English poetry and more than once recites freely from Keats and Shakespeare. The son of a wealthy actor, he could have led an easy life depending on the revenues of his inherited fortune, but he has never taken up a profession and has squandered his money on women and gambling. At the source of this prodigal career we discover an embarrassing Oedipus complex, which reveals that Tyrone has never fully grown up. I quote at some length another passage from Doris Falk's book, because her description of the complex is precise and spares us the trouble of repeating in extenso a psychological situation which we shall discover to be only of ephemeral significance for the meaning of the whole play. At the same time it summarizes Tyrone's past as well as his conduct during the play:

> He is probably the least dramatic of any of O'Neill's protagonists. His role in the play is one long self-analysis, one endless case-history of self-hatred, alienation, neurotic conflict—all within the Oedipus configuration . . . In his sodden conversations with Josie he alternates between the coarse cruelty of a disillusioned lecher and the sweetness and simplicity of a little boy crying for his mother. Expansive at one moment, submissive at another, he does not know his real identity and withdraws from both self-images into the oblivion of drunkenness and the darkness of the womb—synonymous for him with tomb.

> If the first glimpse of Tyrone reveals his disintegration within the masks of self, the second view of him is a study in self-hatred. . . .

> Tyrone explains his guilt to Josie and to himself in terms of his lifelong hatred of his father and love and guilty longing for his mother. During his father's lifetime Tyrone was a drunkard and a ne'er-do-well, but after his father's death he stopped drinking for his mother's sake. "It made me happy to do it. For her. Because she was all I had, all I cared about. Because I loved her."

> Then his mother became ill, and when Tyrone knew she was dying he turned to alcohol again: "I know damned well just before she died she recognized me. She saw I was drunk. Then she closed her eyes so she couldn't see, and was glad to die."

> With his mother's death, all purpose and value departed from Tyrone's life, leaving him incapable of emotion, even of grief.

He travelled across the country by train with his mother's body "in the baggage coach ahead", and spent his drunken nights with a prostitute he had picked up. Tyrone reduces his motives for this debauchery to vengeance upon his mother for leaving him. From that time on his life has been one long effort to obliterate his guilt and to punish himself not only for his behaviour toward his mother, but for his feelings toward her, with their unconscious overtones of incest and hatred.

In Josie Tyrone discovers a woman to substitute for his mother when he revisits the farm he has inherited. The reason for this visit (apparently he spends most of his time in New York) is only hinted at: first we hear that the allowance he still draws from his father's fortune is too small to enable him to lead a comfortable Broadway life. He may have come to collect the rent which Hogan has failed to pay in time. But he may also intend to sell the farm to Hogan, as he had promised before—he has already made sure of his brother's consent (there are only two brief references to Edmund, Tyrone's brother, in *LDJN*). The latter assumption is the more likely since Tyrone expects his farm to be out of probate any day. Whatever his motive, Jim Tyrone has settled in a neighbouring tavern, and Josie and her father notice that his visits have become more and more frequent. Josie tries to make herself believe that Tyrone has no other intention than to forget his misery in the presence of his friends. But she and Hogan cannot help noticing that he is not merely looking for a change: he has cast an eye on Josie. The following is one of Hogan's early remarks: "If you think Jim hasn't been taking in your fine points, you're a fool." In fact, when Tyrone at last arrives late at night for his appointment with Josie, his only wish is to find peace and forgiveness in Josie's arms. Doris Falk explains:

> That same wronged maternal ghost who cried for vindication in *Desire Under the Elms* and *Mourning Becomes Electra* must here again be laid to rest. In Josie's maternal and redemptive love for him Tyrone at last finds forgiveness and release. When he has confessed to Josie and discovers that he is still loved in spite of the hateful self he has revealed in the confession, Tyrone is absolved. The maternal spirit has been placated; now Tyrone can sleep, now he can die.

It is important to note that in this passage Josie appears only as a projection of Tyrone's mind. The question of love is only tackled from Tyrone's point of view, Josie is not treated as a character in her own right. This is why Falk can conclude her argument:

> Tyrone is O'Neill's last little boy lost, crying for his mother.
> Whether or not he actually portrays James O'Neill, Jr., the
> relationship between him and Josie was O'Neill's final bitter
> and rather immature comment on the meaning of love.

These sentences reflect the general tenor of most interpretations. [German literary critic, Ueli] Schenker is also aware of
the fact that the play's main theme is love. He asks himself
whether the power of love will be strong enough to surmount
all the obstacles separating Josie and Tyrone. He derives his
answer from a survey of the characters' psychological development synthesized from a systematic survey of their past and
present actions. From this he concludes that love prevails over
materialism (the father's intrigue, Tyrone's love for money),
but is forced to surrender to the forces of the past, of guilt and
contrition. The moonlight romance proves to be a deceptive
illusion, its peace but a fleeting moment of apparent freedom.
Man can find real peace only in death, when he has escaped
the determining forces of origin, milieu and personal past.

JOSIE'S AND TYRONE'S CONNECTION

With the exception of some characters in *IC*, Tyrone unquestionably represents the most obvious victim of determinism
in the late plays. He is undramatic in the sense that he no
longer engages in any serious struggle to achieve a particular aim. His dipsomania and the loss of his mother have
extinguished the last spark of his will, which, to conclude
from his failure in every profession, was never very strong.
We agree with Josie who, at the end of the play, has come to
realize that there is no remedy for him. For even if we could
take it for granted that, from a medical point of view, there is
still a chance that he will recover, Tyrone is unlikely to be
healed because his lack of will-power is obviously innate. We
know from various accounts how deeply O'Neill was affected by his knowledge that no power in the world could alter
his one brother. And he must have been haunted by the question whether there was any meaning in such a wasted life.
We also know that the completion of the two autobiographical plays, both of which he had written in "tears and blood",
gave him much comfort and satisfaction. He had achieved his
aim of understanding the curse which beset his family.
Surely, we are not wrong in assuming that the playwright, in
recapitulating some stages in his brother's career, wanted to
communicate his own findings. Even those critics who can

discover nothing but the realistic representation of the all-prevailing powers of determinism in the play are forced to admit consciously or unconsciously that there is more to the play than that. Schenker's concluding paragraphs are a case in point. Having explained that the tragedy of the characters consists in their being forced to go on living, he maintains that the night has nevertheless been a blessing to the lovers. Does he simply mean that the illusion of love has momentarily eased their misery? Or has Tyrone really been forgiven? Schenker writes:

> Josie's and Jamie's love is real, too. The drama presents a world which lasts for one night only, but which for that time possesses its own particular and authentic reality, the transient nature of which is taken for granted by the misbegotten from the start.

Valid, authentic reality, however, is surely the contrary of illusion, even if that reality is transient like everything else on earth. Schenker's logic fails him in these sentences, and yet they express something that many of O'Neill's admirers have felt, viz. that O'Neill's plays are aglow with a strange beauty and consolation which does not fit a purely pessimistic view of the world. What does this beauty consist of? What hope and consolation does the dramatist offer?

The opinions that come closest to the truth as I see it are to be found in a statement by Mary McCarthy and in a sentence by critic S.K. Winther. Writing on the occasion of the play's first publication, McCarthy comments on the central symbol in the play:

> This moment, in which the bootlegger's daughter discovers that this middle-aged man is really "dead", emotionally speaking—an exhausted mummified child—is a moment of considerable poignancy. The defeat of all human plans and contrivances is suddenly shaped in the picture of the titaness sitting staring at a stage moon with a shriveled male infant drunkenly sleeping at her side. The image of the survivors takes on a certain grotesque epic form: the woman, stage centre, like a gentle beached whale, appears for an instant as the last survivor of the world.

The whole wording of this passage betrays that the critic has been seized by the emotional impact of the scene. The simple events on the stage assume a mythical quality. But it is S.K. Winther who hits the mark when he says: "This whole play must be interpreted as an elegy", thus pointing to the musical qualities of the play.

Chronology

1888

Eugene Gladstone O'Neill is born to Mary Ellen (Ella) Quinlan and her famous actor husband, James O'Neill, in New York City, the third of three sons: first son, James Jr. (Jamie), born 1878; second son, Edmund, born 1883, dies of a childhood disease 1885.

1888–1895

O'Neill and his family tour the country with his father's theater company.

1896–1900

O'Neill attends St. Aloysius, a Catholic boarding school in Riverdale, New York.

1898

Spanish-American War.

1900–1906

O'Neill attends De LaSalle Military Institute, a Catholic boarding school in New York City; graduates from Betts Academy, Stamford, Connecticut.

1901

President William McKinley is assassinated.

1906

O'Neill enters Princeton University but leaves before the end of the first year after a two-week disciplinary suspension.

1907–1908

O'Neill works in New York City for a jewelry supply company.

1909

NAACP is founded; O'Neill marries Kathleen Jenkins, who is pregnant; James O'Neill sends his son to Honduras.

1910

O'Neill returns from Honduras with malaria; he works with his father's road company as an assistant stage manager; son Eugene Jr. born on May 10.

1911

O'Neill sails to Buenos Aires and after a lonely period of near destitution returns to New York City; O'Neill consents to a divorce from Kathleen on grounds of adultery.

1912

O'Neill lives at Jimmy the Priest's, a waterfront dive in New York City, where he attempts suicide; he is hospitalized for tuberculosis at Gaylord Farm Sanatorium, Wallingford, Connecticut, where he commits himself to writing.

1914

Panama Canal opens; World War I begins; O'Neill writes his first produced play, *Bound East for Cardiff.*

1914–1915

O'Neill attends George Pierce Baker's drama workshop at Harvard; moves to Greenwich Village in New York City and befriends artists and intellectuals at a bar named the Hell Hole.

1916

O'Neill joins George Cook and his wife, the playwright Susan Glaspell, at the Wharf Theater, Provincetown, Massachusetts, where they produce *Bound East for Cardiff.*

1917

United States enters World War I; *The Long Voyage Home* is produced at the Playwright's Theatre in New York.

1918

O'Neill marries Agnes Boulton.

1919

Treaty of Versailles ends World War I; Red Scare begins; Agnes and Eugene's son, Shane, is born on October 30.

1920

Women win the right to vote; *Beyond the Horizon* is produced on Broadway and wins the Pulitzer Prize; James O'Neill dies.

1922

Ella O'Neill dies in Los Angeles; Pulitzer Prize is awarded to *Anna Christie.*

1923

James Jr. (Jamie) dies of complications from alcoholism.

1925

O'Neill's daugher, Oona, is born on May 13.

1927

The *Jazz Singer* is the first talking movie.

1928

Pulitzer Prize is awarded to *Strange Interlude.*

1929

Stock market crash begins the Great Depression; Agnes Boulton is granted a divorce on grounds of desertion; O'Neill marries Carlotta Monterey.

1933

Ah, Wilderness!, an O'Neill comedy, becomes the playwright's second biggest success.

1935

Works Progress Administration is formed; Social Security Act is passed.

1936

O'Neill is awarded the Nobel Prize for literature.

1937–1943

O'Neill and Carlotta build Tao House in Danville, California.

1939

World War II begins with the German invasion of Poland.

1941

The Japanese attack Pearl Harbor; the United States enters World War II.

1943

Oona O'Neill marries film comedian Charlie Chaplin.

1944

O'Neill suffers from uncontrollable tremors; Eugene and Carlotta move to San Francisco.

1945

Germany and Japan surrender; the United Nations is founded.

1946

The Iceman Cometh is produced on Broadway; it is the last Broadway play produced in the playwright's lifetime.

1947

A Moon for the Misbegotten opens in Columbus, Ohio; it is the last play to open anywhere during the playwright's lifetime; O'Neill's poor health prevents him from writing.

1949

NATO is founded.

1950

Senator Joseph McCarthy charges that State Department officials are members of the Communist Party; Eugene Jr. commits suicide.

1951

Carlotta suffers breakdown.

1953

O'Neill dies at the Shelton Hotel in Boston on November 27.

1956

Long Day's Journey into Night is produced at the Square Theatre in Greenwich Village, New York City; the play wins O'Neill a fourth Pulitzer Prize.

FOR FURTHER RESEARCH

BIOGRAPHICAL WORKS AND PUBLISHED LETTERS

Travis Bogard and Jackson Bryer, *Selected Letters of Eugene O'Neill.* New Haven, CT: Yale University Press, 1988.

Agnes Boulton, *Part of a Long Story.* Garden City, NY: Doubleday, 1958.

Croswell Bowen, *The Curse of the Misbegotten.* New York: McGraw-Hill, 1960.

Barret Clark, *Eugene O'Neill: The Man and His Plays.* New York: Dover, 1967.

Dorothy Commins, ed., *"Love and Admiration and Respect": The O'Neill-Commins Correspondence.* Durham, NC: Duke University Press, 1986.

Arthur and Barbara Gelb, *O'Neill.* New York: Harper, 1973.

Nancy Roberts and Arthur Roberts, *"As Ever, Gene": The Letters of Eugene O'Neill to George Jean Nathan.* Rutherford, NJ: Fairleigh Dickinson University Press, 1987.

Louis Scheaffer, *O'Neill: Son and Artist.* Boston: Little, Brown, 1973.

ABOUT EUGENE O'NEILL'S PLAYS

Doris Alexander, *The Tempering of Eugene O'Neill.* New York: Harcourt, Brace and World, 1962.

Normand Berlin, *Eugene O'Neill.* New York: Grove Press, 1982.

———, *Eugene O'Neill: Three Plays.* London: MacMillan Education, 1989.

Harold Bloom, ed., *Eugene O'Neill:* The Iceman Cometh. New York: Chelsea House, 1987.

Frederic Carpenter, *Eugene O'Neill.* Boston: Twayne, 1978.

Virginia Floyd, ed., *Eugene O'Neill: The Unfinished Plays.* New York: Ungar Press, 1988.

John Gassner, ed., *O'Neill: A Collection of Critical Essays*. Englewood Cliffs, NJ: Prentice-Hall, 1964.

Ernest Griffin, *Eugene O'Neill: A Collection of Criticism*. New York: McGraw-Hill, 1976.

Michael Hinden, *Long Day's Journey into Night: Native Eloquence*. Boston: Twayne, 1990.

Laurin Porter, *The Banished Prince: Time, Memory, and Ritual in the Late Plays of Eugene O'Neill*. Ann Arbor: U.M.I. Research Press, 1988.

Dhupaty Raghavacharyulu, *Eugene O'Neill: A Study*. Bombay: Popular Prakashan, 1965.

Margaret Ranald, *The Eugene O'Neill Companion*. Westport, CT: Greenwood Press, 1984.

John H. Stroupe, ed., *Critical Approaches to O'Neill*. New York: AMS Press, 1988.

HISTORICAL BACKGROUND

Gerald M. Berkowitz, *American Drama of the Twentieth Century*. London: Longman, 1992.

Gerald Bordman, *The Concise Oxford Companion to American Theatre*. New York: Oxford University Press, 1987.

Oscar G. Brockett, *History of the Theatre*. Boston: Allyn and Bacon, 1987.

Kenneth C. Davis, *Don't Know Much About History*. New York: Avon Books, 1990.

Martin Lamm, *Modern Drama*. New York: Philosophical Library, 1953.

Frederick Lumley, *Trends in 20th Century Drama*. New York: Oxford University Press, 1960.

David W. Sievers, *Freud on Broadway: A History of Psychoanalysis and the American Drama*. New York: Hermitage House, 1955.

Ronald Wainscott, *Staging O'Neill: The Experimental Years, 1920–1934*. New Haven, CT: Yale University Press, 1988.

G.J. Watson, *Drama: An Introduction*. New York: St. Martin's Press, 1983.

G.B. Wilson, *Three Hundred Years of American Drama and Theatre*. Englewood Cliffs, NJ: Prentice-Hall, 1973.

Works by Eugene O'Neill

Eugene O'Neill's works are available in a wide variety of anthologies and reissues; therefore, facts of publication are omitted from the following list of produced plays. The date listed is the year the play was written.

Thirst (1913)

Fog (1914)

Bound East for Cardiff (1914)

Abortion (1914)

The Movie Man (1914)

The Sniper (1915)

Before Breakfast (1916)

In the Zone (1917)

Ile (1917)

The Long Voyage Home (1917)

The Moon of the Caribbees (1917)

The Rope (1918)

Beyond the Horizon (1918)

The Dreamy Kid (1918)

Where the Cross Is Made (1918)

The Straw (1919)

Chris Christopherson (1919)

Gold (1920)

Anna Christie (1920)

The Emperor Jones (1920)

Diff'rent (1920)

The First Man (1921)

The Hairy Ape (1921)

The Fountain (1922)

Welded (1923)

All God's Chillun Got Wings (1923)

The Ancient Mariner (1923)

Desire Under the Elms (1924)

Marco Millions (1925)

The Great God Brown (1925)

Lazarus Laughed (1926)

Strange Interlude (1927)

Dynamo (1928)

Mourning Becomes Electra (1931)

Ah, Wilderness! (1932)

Days Without End (1933)

The Iceman Cometh (1939)

More Stately Mansions (1941)

Long Day's Journey into Night (1941)

Hughie (1941)

A Touch of the Poet (1942)

A Moon for the Misbegotten (1943)

INDEX

never attended, 34
production of plays, 32-36
reaction to father's theater, 30,
    45, 82
shunned, 25
and religion
    comments on, 54, 84, 112-13
    Irish Catholicism, 69, 78, 83,
    97
    lack of, 78, 79
    Puritanism, 69, 73, 82
    on relationship between man
    and God, 84-85, 97, 112
    symbolism, 117
    treatment of, 112-19
revival of plays, 73-74, 80-81
suicide attempt of, 19, 52, 128
techniques, theatrical, 50
    distortion in setting and ges-
    ture, 42
    expressionism, 81-82, 89-95
    fantastic plot, 43
    humor, 25, 27, 49
    internal monologues, 45, 47,
    50, 86
    masks, 42, 45, 47, 86, 114
    mythology, 45, 48-49
    psychological naturalism, 27,
    56-57, 75, 77
    realism, 42, 82, 84, 90
    sound effects, 42, 91-92, 104
    theatrical design, 47-48, 50, 81,
    91-93
on the United States, 76-77
view of women, 50, 56, 60, 65
work experience, 18-19
work habits, 20, 21-22, 24-25
writing tragedy, 27, 50, 54-56,
    76-78, 85-87
O'Neill, Eugene Gladstone Jr.
    (son), 18, 22-23, 52, 159
O'Neill, James (father), 15-17, 18,
    20, 29, 50
O'Neill, James, Jr. (Jamie,
    brother), 14, 16-18, 20-21, 26
O'Neill, Oona (daughter), 20, 22-
    24
O'Neill, Shane Rudraighe (son),
    20, 22-24, 159

Part of a Long Story (Boulton), 22
Personal Equation, The, 46
Pirandello, Luigi, 52

Pitt-Smith, Richard. *See* O'Neill,
    Eugene Gladstone Jr.
Poe, Edgar Allan, 82
Porter, Laurin, 67
Princeton University, 17-18
"The Progression of Alcoholism
    and the Family" (Howards),
    149-51
Provincetown Players, 19, 21, 31-
    33, 46, 75, 104
Pulitzer Prize, 14, 20, 21, 26, 38,
    40, 53
Puritanism, 55-56, 69, 73, 82, 99,
    121-26

Quinn, Arthur Hobson, 54

Raleigh, John Henry, 82, 103
Ranald, Margaret Loftus, 45
realism, 42, 82, 84, 90
Reckoning, The, 46
Rice, Elmer, 81
Rope, 33
Royal Dramatic Theatre, 26, 39
Rubaiyat (Khayámm), 132, 133

Sandy, Sarah, 16
Scarlet Letter, The, (Hawthorne)
    68
Scheibler, Rolf, 170
Schenker, Ueli, 176-77
Schnitzler, Arthur, 30
Servitude, 49, 64
Shakespeare, William, 83, 85
Sharp, William L., 41
Shaw, George Bernard, 30, 41,
    52, 83, 101
Smart Set, plays published in, 20
Sophocles, 78
Speyer, James, 24
S.S. Glencairn, 141
St. Aloysius School (New York
    City), 17
Strange Interlude
    Charlie Marsden, 131
    critics on, 41, 77
    interior monologue in, 48
    Nina, 63
    as novelistic, 35
    Pulitzer Prize for, 21
    themes in, 48, 53
Straw, The, 36, 133
Streetcar Named Desire